SWIPESOBER: THE ART OF DIGITAL WELLNESS

Milap Oza

Chennai • Bangalore

CLEVER FOX PUBLISHING
Chennai, India

Published by CLEVER FOX PUBLISHING 2025

ISBN: 978-93-6707-232-5

Dedication

To my Mummy and Papa,

your blessings have been my silent strength—flawless, pure, and always present, even in moments when I doubted myself. This book is a reflection of the values you've instilled in me.

To Yogita,

my partner in every sense—thank you for standing beside me with patience, faith, and love through every high and low. Your quiet strength has been my anchor.

And to my son, Vedaarth,

your smile, your questions, your very presence—remind me why purpose matters. You are my truest inspiration and the light that keeps me moving forward.

Thanks to all my well-wishers

whose encouragement, belief, and kind words have added warmth to this journey.

CONTENTS

PREFACE

In a world where digital screens have become our constant companions, we are witnessing a silent transformation, one that turns us into mindless consumers of information, endlessly scrolling, swiping, and tapping. Smartphones, once hailed as tools of progress, have now become shackles that strip us of our focus, creativity, and even our ability to be present in the moment.

Children, who should be discovering the wonders of the real world, are instead glued to screens, lost in a virtual universe. Adults, who once enjoyed deep conversations and meaningful interactions, now spend hours consumed by endless notifications, social media feeds, and digital distractions. The price we pay is enormous: declining mental health, fractured relationships, reduced productivity, and a life devoid of true purpose and mindfulness.

This book is a wake-up call: a guide to breaking free from the invisible chains of digital addiction. Whether you are a child, a teenager, or an adult, it will help you recognize signs of excessive screen dependency, understand the underlying psychological traps, and provide practical steps to regain your time, focus, and well-being.

Through a combination of research, real-life experiences, and actionable strategies, this book aims to help you regain control of your digital habits and reconnect with the world around you. Imagine a life where you are not a slave to your phone, where your mind is free to think, create, and truly live. That life is possible, and this book will show you how to achieve it.

It is time to step out of the digital fog and into a world of clarity, presence, and purpose. Let's embark on this journey together, toward a life of balance, fulfillment, and true human connection.

How This Book is Structured

To help you systematically overcome digital addiction and reclaim your life, this book is divided into three parts:

Part 1: Understanding the Addiction

In this section, we explore how and why digital addiction has taken hold of our lives. We examine the psychological, neurological, and societal aspects of addiction to smartphones, the Internet, and social networks. Through self-assessments and real-life examples, you will identify whether you or your loved ones are affected and understand the hidden mechanisms that keep you hooked.

Part 2: Breaking Free from the Digital Chains

Once the problem is recognized, the next step is to take control. This section provides practical strategies to reduce screen time, set digital boundaries, and regain your focus. You will learn about digital minimalism, detoxing from social media, and rewiring your brain to resist compulsive usage. These steps will empower you to break free from technology's grip and reclaim your mental clarity and well-being.

Part 3: Embracing a New Lifestyle

Digital detox is not just about cutting back—it's about replacing harmful habits with meaningful, fulfilling ones. This final section will help you cultivate real-world connections, rediscover offline hobbies, and embrace a balanced, tech-healthy lifestyle. Whether you're a parent raising tech-smart kids, a professional seeking better focus, or someone simply longing for a more present and mindful life, this section will guide you toward a sustainable and rewarding digital detox journey.

This book is more than just a guide; it is a movement to reclaim the best version of ourselves. Let's begin the journey together.

– Milap Oza

ABOUT THE AUTHOR

Milap Dilipkumar Oza is an Information security professional & columnist with an experience of over a decade, working on a mission to reshape our relationship with technology. With 14 years of experience in information security, he has worked with leading financial and telecom giants, trained hundreds of professionals on cybersecurity awareness and digital best practices. But his work isn't just about preventing cyber threats—it's about making people conscious users of technology.

Over the years, Milap noticed an unsettling trend: People love technology, they chase the latest gadgets, and they proudly show off their fancy smartphones—yet very few think about *how* they're using them. Scrolling endlessly at dinner tables, staring at screens in parks, mindlessly checking notifications during important conversations—these behaviors became the new normal. Society was changing, and not necessarily for the better.

At first, he thought, *Well, to each their own*. But then, one day, he looked around and saw something that shook him. Kids—tiny, bright-eyed, full-of-energy kids—are completely glued to their screens. Instead of running around, climbing trees, or playing tag, they were motionless, hypnotized by their devices, lost in a digital abyss. Parks had become silent. Family functions felt like everyone was there physically but absent mentally. Even toddlers were throwing tantrums without their screens. That was the trigger. That was the moment he knew he *had* to do something.

Determined to bring back mindful tech use, he founded Swipesober (www.swipesober.com), an initiative designed to help people break free from smart phone addiction and reclaim their lives. Through this platform, he shares strategies, research, and stories to inspire people to wake up from their digital daze and start living *fully aware*.

In addition to running awareness campaigns and training professionals, Milap has written multiple articles on cybersecurity, digital wellness, and the hidden dangers of overusing technology. Currently, he is working on a book about digital detox, blending research, self-help strategies, and personal experiences to guide readers toward a healthier, more intentional relationship with technology.

When he's not writing or teaching, you might find him observing society's tech habits (probably judging a little), advocating for mindful living, or secretly hoping people remember that life exists beyond their screens.

PART 1

UNDERSTANDING THE ADDICTION

1. The Digital Trap: How We Got Here – The rise of smartphones, social media, and internet dependency.
2. Are You Addicted? – Signs, symptoms, and self-assessment to identify screen addiction.
3. The Science Behind Digital Addiction – How screens hijack our brains, dopamine loops, and behavioral conditioning.
4. The Dark Side of social media & the Internet – Manipulation, misinformation, and psychological impact.
5. Children & Screens: A Lost Childhood? – How screen addiction affects children's brain development, learning, and behavior.
6. The Teenage Digital Dilemma – Social validation, cyberbullying, and mental health concerns.
7. Adults & Digital Burnout – Productivity loss, stress, and how digital addiction ruins personal and professional life.
8. The Physical Toll of Digital Overuse – Eye strain, sleep disorders, and posture-related health issues.
9. Family & Relationships in the Digital Age – How excessive screen time is affecting personal bonds.
10. The Corporate & Workplace Digital Addiction – How work-related digital overload is impacting efficiency and mental well-being

CHAPTER 1

THE DIGITAL TRAP – HOW WE GOT HERE

At the beginning of the 21st century, the world stood on the brink of a digital revolution. The internet, once a simple tool for research and communication, had begun to weave itself into the fabric of our daily lives. In just two decades, we went from dial-up connections and bulky computers to sleek, pocket-sized devices that hold the entire world at our fingertips.

The rise of smartphones, social media, and constant internet access was supposed to make life easier, more connected, and more productive. Instead, it has left us overstimulated, distracted, and, in many cases, addicted. What was once a tool for convenience has become a crutch we can't seem to put down. This chapter explores how we got here—how technology, designed to serve us, ended up controlling us.

The Smartphone Revolution: A Double-Edged Sword

The launch of the iPhone in 2007 was a turning point in human history. It wasn't just a phone; it was a powerful computer, a camera, a music player, a GPS, and a gateway to an endless stream of information—all in the palm of our hands. Other tech giants followed suit, flooding the market with high-tech, ultra-responsive devices that seamlessly integrated into our lives.

At first, smartphones were marketed as tools of productivity. They allowed us to send emails on the go, browse the web, and navigate new cities with ease. But as app developers and tech companies recognized the potential for profit, the focus shifted. Instead of merely helping us perform tasks efficiently, smartphones were designed to keep us engaged constantly.

Every notification, every buzz, every colorful app icon was meticulously crafted to draw us back in. The smartphone was no longer just a tool; it was a habit-forming device.

The Social Media Takeover

Then came social media—the digital wildfire that reshaped how we communicate, share, and consume information. Platforms like Facebook, Instagram, Twitter, and later TikTok were built with a simple goal: to keep users online as long as possible.

To achieve this, tech companies turned to behavioral psychology, employing strategies that hijacked the human brain's reward system:

- **Infinite Scrolling** – A never-ending stream of content designed to prevent users from stopping.
- **Likes and Comments** – Instant validation that fuels our need for social approval.
- **Personalized Feeds** – Algorithms that track our behavior to show us content tailored to our interests, keeping us engaged longer.
- **Push Notifications** – Constant digital nudges pulling us back in, even when we're not actively using the app.

The result? A society glued to screens, endlessly scrolling, comparing, and seeking approval. Social media shifted from being a fun way to connect with friends to a psychological battlefield where attention is the most valuable currency.

Internet Dependency: Always Connected, Never Present

The internet, which once required effort to assess, is now available anytime, anywhere. With a few taps, we can enter an online world filled with endless entertainment, information, and social interactions. While this has undeniable benefits, it has also blurred the boundaries between work and leisure, between the digital world and reality.

- **The 24/7 Work Culture** – Employees are expected to be reachable at all times, leading to stress and burnout.
- **The Death of Boredom** – Moments of quiet reflection have been replaced by the need to check our phones every spare second.
- **Shortened Attention Spans** – Constantly switching between apps, videos, and messages has rewired our brains, making it harder to focus on any one task.

The Digital Trap: Why We Keep Coming Back

Despite knowing the downsides, we keep reaching for our devices. Why? Because our brains have been trained to crave the instant gratification they provide. Every time we receive a notification, our brain releases dopamine—the same chemical linked to addiction. Over time, this reinforcement creates a compulsive cycle, making it difficult to resist the urge to check our phones.

The digital world thrives on our attention, and tech companies spend billions designing products that keep us engaged. The longer we stay online, the more data they collect, the more ads they show, and the more money they make.

Breaking Free: Acknowledging the Problem

The first step to escaping the digital trap is recognizing that we are caught in it. Our relationship with technology needs to shift from **mindless consumption to mindful use**. Smartphones, social media, and the internet are not inherently bad—but when left unchecked, they can take over our lives.

This book will guide you through that transformation—helping you break free from digital addiction, regain control of your time, and reconnect with the real world. The choice is yours: Will you continue to be a passive user, or will you take charge of your digital habits and reclaim your focus, creativity, and peace of mind?

The journey to digital freedom begins now.

ARE YOU ADDICTED?

Signs, Symptoms, and Self-Assessment to Identify Screen Addiction

> *"The chains of habit are too weak to be felt until they are too strong to be broken."*
>
> – **Samuel Johnson**

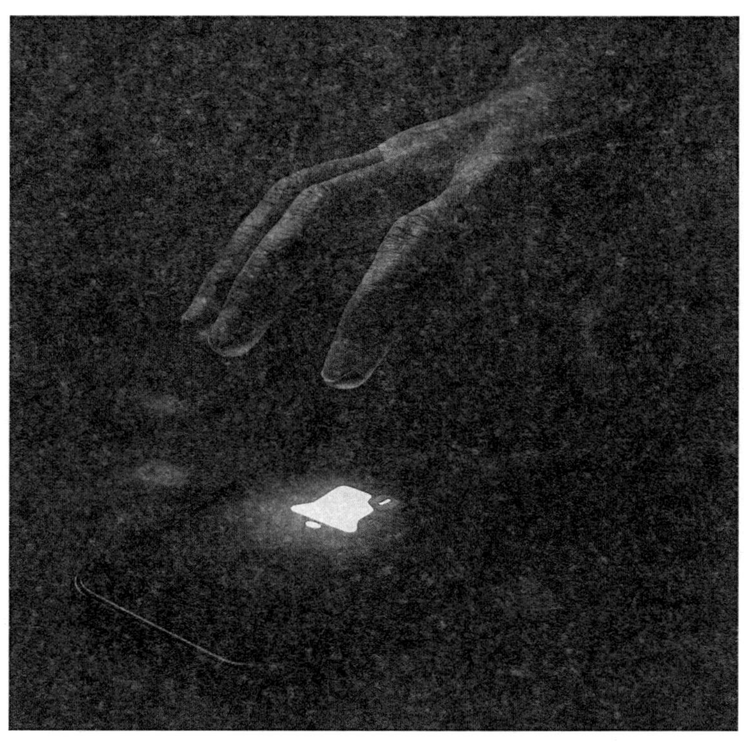

Technology has become so deeply woven into our daily routines that we often fail to recognize when our use crosses the line from convenience to dependency. While smartphones, social media, and the internet provide undeniable benefits, they can also lead to excessive usage, harming our mental and physical well-being.

But how do you know if you're truly addicted? The first step to breaking free is identifying whether your screen use is healthy or if it's controlling you. This chapter will help you recognize the signs of screen addiction, understand the symptoms, and take a self-assessment to evaluate your relationship with digital devices.

Understanding Screen Addiction

Screen addiction—also called digital addiction or problematic technology use—is a compulsive dependence on smartphones, social media, gaming, or the internet, leading to a loss of control over screen time. Like other forms of addiction, it triggers dopamine release in the brain, reinforcing behavior that can be hard to break.

The problem isn't just how much time we spend on screens, but how they interfere with our lives—affecting our productivity, mental health, sleep, and real-world relationships.

Signs of Screen Addiction

If you're wondering whether your phone or internet use is excessive, ask yourself if you relate to any of these common signs of screen addiction:

1. You Check Your Phone Constantly

- Do you reach for your phone first thing in the morning and last thing at night?

- Do you check your phone even when there are no notifications?
- Do you feel uneasy or anxious when you don't have access to your phone?

2. You Lose Track of Time Online

- Do you plan to use your phone for "just a few minutes" but end up spending hours?
- Do you get caught in endless scrolling, unable to stop?
- Have you ever neglected responsibilities because of screen time?

3. You Prioritize Screens Over Real-Life Interactions

- Do you find yourself texting or scrolling even during face-to-face conversations?
- Do you prefer online interactions over spending time with family or friends in person?
- Have your relationships suffered because of too much screen time?

4. You Feel Anxious Without Your Phone

- Do you panic if you forget your phone at home?
- Do you experience FOMO (Fear of Missing Out) when you're offline?
- Do you feel the urge to check social media or messages every few minutes?

5. You Struggle to Focus on Tasks

- Do you get easily distracted by notifications when working or studying?
- Do you constantly switch between apps and struggle to concentrate?
- Has your attention span become shorter over time?

6. Your Sleep is Disrupted

- Do you use screens right before bed?
- Do you struggle to fall asleep because of late-night scrolling?
- Do you wake up feeling tired even after a full night's sleep?

7. **You Use Screens as an Escape**
   - Do you turn to your phone whenever you feel bored, lonely, or stressed?
   - Do you use social media or gaming to avoid real-life problems?
   - Do you feel uneasy when you're not occupied with a screen?

Self-Assessment: Are You Addicted?

Take this quick self-assessment to measure your level of screen dependence. Answer Yes or No to each statement.

1. I often spend more time on my phone or computer than I originally intended.
2. I feel anxious or uncomfortable when I don't have access to my phone or the internet.
3. I frequently check my phone, even when I don't receive a notification.
4. I have neglected work, studies, or responsibilities because of excessive screen use.
5. My screen time has affected my sleep schedule and overall rest.
6. I prefer digital interactions over face-to-face conversations.
7. I use my phone or social media to cope with stress, anxiety, or boredom.
8. I feel distracted and struggle to focus because of constant screen use.
9. I've tried to reduce my screen time, but I always end up going back to my old habits.
10. People close to me have commented on my excessive screen use.

Results:

- **0-3 Yes Answers**: You have a healthy relationship with technology. Keep maintaining balance.
- **4-6 Yes Answers**: You may have a moderate dependence on screens. Consider setting boundaries to prevent addiction.
- **7-10 Yes Answers**: You show strong signs of screen addiction. It's time to take serious action and regain control.

What's Next?

Recognizing the problem is the first step toward change. If you find yourself struggling with digital dependency, don't worry—you're not alone. The next chapters will help you understand why you're addicted, how technology is designed to keep you hooked, and practical ways to break free from excessive screen time.

By regaining control of your digital habits, you can reclaim your time, mental clarity, and real-world connections. The goal is not to eliminate technology from your life but to use it intentionally—so it serves you, rather than controls you.

Let's move forward and explore the psychology behind digital addiction—so you can break free and live a more mindful, present, and fulfilling life.

THE SCIENCE BEHIND DIGITAL ADDICTION

How Screens Hijack Our Brains, Dopamine Loops, and Behavioral Conditioning

> *"Nothing vast enters the life of mortals without a curse."*
>
> – **Sophocles**

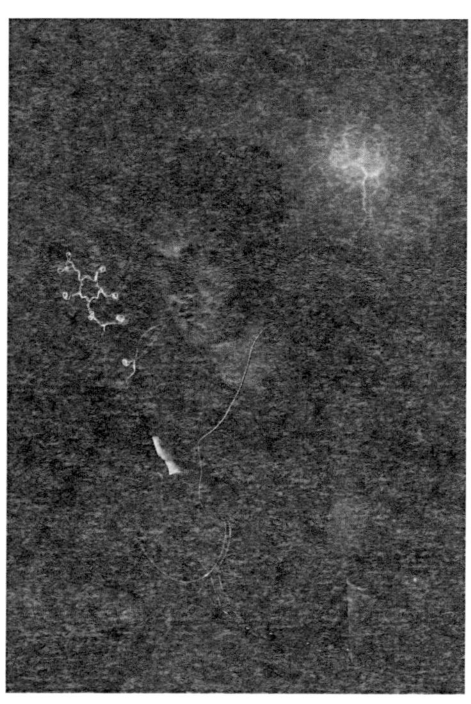

Every time you pick up your phone to check a notification, scroll through social media, or play a mobile game, your brain is undergoing a complex neurological process—one designed to keep you hooked. Digital addiction isn't just a bad habit; it's the result of neuroscience, psychology, and behavioral conditioning working together to trap us in a cycle of endless screen use.

Why is it so hard to put our phones down? Why do we feel the urge to check for updates, even when we know there's nothing urgent? The answer lies in the way technology hijacks our brain's reward system, creating a cycle of dopamine-driven reinforcement that keeps us glued to our screens.

This chapter breaks down the science of digital addiction, explaining how tech companies use psychological tricks to capture our attention—and what we can do to break free.

How Screens Hijack Our Brains

At the core of digital addiction is dopamine, a neurotransmitter responsible for motivation, pleasure, and reinforcement of behaviors. Dopamine is released in response to rewarding activities—such as eating delicious food, exercising, or receiving praise. But modern technology has learned to hack this system, creating artificial bursts of dopamine that make us crave more screen time.

The Dopamine Loop: Why You Can't Stop Scrolling

Every time you get a like, a comment, or a new notification, your brain releases dopamine, making you feel good. This positive reinforcement creates a loop:

1. **Trigger** – A notification pops up, a new post appears, or an autoplay video begins.
2. **Action** – You check your phone, scroll through content, or watch a short clip.
3. **Reward** – Your brain releases dopamine, making you feel satisfied.
4. **Reinforcement** – You associate screen use with pleasure, making you more likely to repeat the behavior.

Tech companies intentionally design apps to exploit this loop. Features like infinite scrolling, autoplay videos, and random notifications ensure that you keep coming back for more—without even realizing it.

Behavioral Conditioning: How Tech Keeps Us Hooked

The addictive nature of digital devices isn't accidental. It's the result of careful behavioral design based on psychological principles that keep users engaged. Here are some of the most effective methods used to increase screen time:

1. Variable Rewards (The Slot Machine Effect)

Psychologists have found that unpredictable rewards are far more addictive than consistent rewards. This is why:

- Scrolling through social media is like pulling the lever on a slot machine—you never know when you'll see something exciting.
- Opening an app like Instagram or TikTok presents new, unpredictable content each time, keeping you engaged.

- Refreshing your feed, checking emails, or reading news updates feeds the anticipation of something new.

This randomness is what makes it nearly impossible to stop. The possibility of seeing something rewarding keeps us scrolling.

2. The Fear of Missing Out (FOMO)

Social media plays on our innate fear of being left out of important events, trends, or conversations. The constant stream of updates makes us feel like we must stay connected, or we'll miss something significant.

- Stories and disappearing content (like Snapchat or Instagram Stories) pressure users to check in frequently before the content vanishes.
- Trending topics and viral challenges create a sense of urgency—making users feel like they need to participate to stay relevant.

3. Infinite Scrolling and Autoplay

Apps like TikTok, Instagram, and YouTube remove natural stopping points, making it easier to consume content for hours:

- **Infinite Scrolling** – Instead of needing to refresh, new posts keep appearing endlessly, preventing users from stopping.
- **Autoplay Videos** – Instead of giving you a break, the next video plays automatically, pushing you deeper into the content rabbit hole.
- **Suggested Content** – Algorithms track your preferences and curate personalized recommendations, ensuring that every video, post, or article is something you'll likely enjoy.

Without a natural endpoint, people lose track of time—often spending hours online without realizing it.

4. Social Validation and Digital Approval

Humans are wired to seek approval from others. Social media exploits this need for validation by turning likes, comments, and shares into digital rewards.

- The more likes a post receives, the more dopamine is released—making people crave more interactions.
- Seeing other people's engagement makes users feel pressured to post more frequently, leading to increased app usage.
- Notifications act as instant gratification, making us feel important and valued whenever our phone buzzes.

This system creates a cycle of validation-seeking, where users become dependent on social media for self-worth.

The Long-Term Effects of Digital Addiction

While the short-term effects of excessive screen use might seem harmless, over time, digital addiction can reshape the brain, leading to:

Reduced Attention Span – The constant switching between apps and notifications weakens our ability to focus on one task for an extended period.

Increased Anxiety and Depression – Studies have shown that excessive social media use can lead to higher levels of stress, anxiety, and self-comparison, reducing overall mental well-being.

Weakened Real-Life Connections – As digital interactions replace face-to-face conversations, many people feel disconnected from real relationships and struggle with social skills.

Poor Sleep Quality – The blue light from screens interferes with melatonin production, causing insomnia, fatigue, and disrupted sleep cycles.

Overstimulation and Burnout – Constant exposure to digital content overloads the brain, making it harder to experience joy in simple, real-world activities.

Breaking Free: Understanding the Addiction Is the First Step

Now that you understand how digital addiction works, the next step is taking control of your screen habits. The good news? You have the power to break the cycle.

- **Recognizing the triggers** – Become aware of the psychological tricks that keep you engaged.

- **Setting boundaries** – Limit notifications, screen time, and social media use.
- **Replacing digital habits with real-world activities** – Find alternative ways to get dopamine—exercise, hobbies, or spending time with loved ones.
- **Practicing mindful technology use** – Use screens with intention, rather than mindless scrolling.

Technology itself isn't the enemy—it's how we use it that matters. By understanding the science behind digital addiction, we can reclaim our focus, productivity, and real-life happiness.

Are you ready to break free? The next chapter will guide you through practical strategies to detox from digital addiction and regain control over your life.

THE DARK SIDE OF SOCIAL MEDIA & THE INTERNET

Manipulation, Misinformation, and Psychological Impact

> *"Nothing in the world is more dangerous than sincere ignorance and conscientious stupidity."*
>
> **– Martin Luther King Jr.**

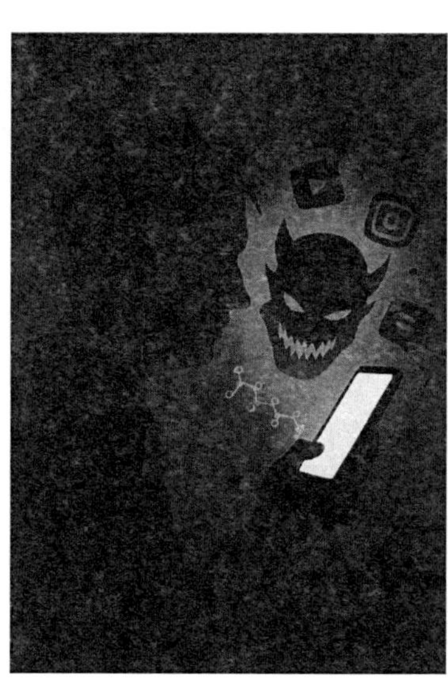

The internet was once hailed as the ultimate tool for knowledge, communication, and global connection. But beneath its shiny surface lies a dark and manipulative world that shapes thoughts, spreads misinformation, and influences behavior—often without users even realizing it.

Social media, in particular, has transformed from a space for connection into a powerful tool for control, used by corporations, political entities, and influencers to manipulate public perception. The platforms we use every day—Facebook, Instagram, TikTok, YouTube, Twitter—are not just passive networks; they are highly engineered ecosystems designed to keep us engaged, influence our decisions, and profit from our data.

In this chapter, we will uncover the hidden dangers of social media and the internet, from misinformation and propaganda to the profound psychological effects it has on individuals and society as a whole.

1. The Business of Manipulation: How Social Media Controls You

Social media companies do not make money when you use their platforms; they make money when you stay on them. Their entire business model is based on maximizing your screen time and keeping you addicted.

The Algorithm Knows You Better Than You Know Yourself

- Every click, like, share, and comment is tracked.
- AI-powered algorithms analyze your behavior to serve content that keeps you engaged.
- If you like one conspiracy video, the algorithm feeds you more extreme content, pushing you deeper into an echo chamber.

The Attention Economy: You Are the Product

- Advertisers pay billions to social media companies to target users based on their online behavior.
- Your personal data—your preferences, search history, and even your fears—is sold to advertisers.
- Social media is not free; you pay for it with your time, attention, and personal information.

Addiction by Design: The Psychological Hooks of Social Media

- Infinite scrolling ensures you never reach the end of the content.
- Autoplay videos keep you watching without thinking.
- Likes and notifications trigger dopamine hits, keeping you addicted.

The result? You are no longer in control of your attention—social media companies are.

2. The Epidemic of Misinformation & Fake News

The internet was supposed to democratize information, but instead, it has become a battlefield of lies, half-truths, and propaganda.

Fake News Travels Faster Than Facts

- Studies show that false information spreads six times faster than the truth on social media.
- Sensational headlines and emotionally charged content get more engagement, making them more likely to be promoted by algorithms.

Deepfakes & Manipulated Content

- AI-generated videos can create convincing but fake news, making it difficult to tell what's real.

- Images and quotes are easily edited to mislead and manipulate public perception.

Echo Chambers & Polarization

- Social media feeds only show you content that aligns with your beliefs, reinforcing your opinions and limiting exposure to opposing viewpoints.
- This creates ideological bubbles, where misinformation flourishes unchecked.

Weaponization of Misinformation

- Political groups, corporations, and even governments use bots, trolls, and fake accounts to manipulate public opinion.
- Many viral trends, movements, and narratives are not organic—they are manufactured to serve an agenda.

The consequence? A misinformed society that is easier to control, divide, and manipulate.

3. The Psychological Impact: How Social Media Is Hurting You

Beyond manipulation and misinformation, social media has a direct and devastating impact on mental health. The way we consume digital content affects our emotions, self-esteem, and even our brain chemistry.

Comparison Culture: The Illusion of Perfection

- Social media only shows the highlights of people's lives, creating unrealistic expectations.
- Seeing curated, edited, and filtered images leads to self-doubt, low self-esteem, and depression.

- Studies show that excessive social media use is linked to higher rates of anxiety, loneliness, and dissatisfaction with life.

The Rise of Cyberbullying & Online Hate

- Online anonymity emboldens people to harass, insult, and spread hate without consequence.
- Victims of cyberbullying experience increased stress, anxiety, and even suicidal thoughts.
- Cancel culture and online shaming create fear, anxiety, and extreme social pressure.

Attention Fragmentation & Cognitive Decline

- Social media trains your brain for short-term engagement, reducing your ability to focus on deep work.
- The constant influx of information lowers attention spans, making it harder to read, learn, and retain knowledge.

Dopamine Addiction & Emotional Rollercoaster

- Social media creates an artificial cycle of highs and lows, where you crave validation through likes and comments.
- The lack of engagement can trigger feelings of rejection, sadness, and inadequacy.
- Over time, social media addiction rewires the brain, making real-life interactions less fulfilling than digital ones.

4. Breaking Free: How to Regain Control Over Your Mind

Now that you understand the dark side of social media and the internet, the question is: What can you do about it?

Be Mindful of Your Consumption

- Question everything you see online. Who benefits from this information?
- Use fact-checking websites before believing or sharing news.

Limit Your Social Media Usage

- Turn off unnecessary notifications to reduce distractions.
- Use apps that track and limit your screen time.

Escape the Algorithm

- Follow diverse sources of information to break out of your echo chamber.
- Seek out long-form content, books, and deep discussions instead of short, viral posts.

Detox Your Digital Life

- Take regular breaks from social media and engage in real-world activities.
- Prioritize face-to-face interactions over online communication.

Be Conscious of Manipulation Tactics

- Recognize that social media platforms are designed to keep you addicted.
- Ask yourself: Am I using technology, or is technology using me?

Learning: Reclaiming Your Mind

The internet and social media are not inherently evil—but the way they are designed and used today is dangerous. They manipulate emotions, distort reality, and exploit human psychology for profit and control.

The key is awareness and intentional use. Instead of being a passive consumer, be a conscious digital user. The more control you regain over your online habits, the more power you reclaim over your mind, well-being, and freedom.

Are you ready to step out of the digital illusion and start living with clarity and purpose? The next chapter will guide you toward a practical digital detox, helping you reset your relationship with technology and reclaim your focus, peace, and real-world connection.

CHILDREN & SCREENS: A LOST CHILDHOOD?

How Screen Addiction Affects Brain Development, Learning, and Behavior

> *"The more high-tech we become, the more nature we need."*
>
> **– Richard Louv**

In the past, childhood was filled with outdoor adventures, imaginative play, and face-to-face social interactions. Today, it's increasingly dominated by glowing screens, endless YouTube videos, addictive mobile games, and social media scrolling. The digital world has replaced playgrounds, books, and real-world experiences—raising the question: Are we losing childhood to screens?

Children today are growing up in a hyper-connected world where digital devices are their primary source of entertainment, education, and socialization. While technology can be a valuable tool, its excessive and uncontrolled use is leading to alarming consequences for brain development, learning abilities, and emotional well-being.

This chapter explores how screen addiction is rewiring children's brains, altering their behavior, and reshaping the future of an entire generation—and what parents, educators, and society must do to prevent it.

1. The Developing Brain: How Screens Are Rewiring Childhood

Children's brains are highly plastic, meaning they are constantly forming new connections based on their experiences. Unlike previous generations, today's kids are growing up with screens as their primary source of stimulation, affecting their cognitive, emotional, and social development.

Screens vs. Real-World Experiences

Reduced Attention Span & Focus

- Studies show that excessive screen time weakens the brain's ability to focus for long periods.

- Fast-paced content, quick cuts, and constant notifications train children's brains for short bursts of attention, making deep focus on tasks like reading or studying difficult.

Delayed Language and Social Skills

- Face-to-face interactions are essential for developing speech, communication, and emotional intelligence.
- Children who spend excessive time on screens show delayed language development and weaker social skills due to reduced real-world conversations.

Overstimulation & Emotional Dysregulation

- Bright screens, fast-moving animations, and rapid dopamine hits overstimulate young brains, making real-world activities seem dull in comparison.
- This leads to emotional outbursts, frustration, and decreased patience when children are not entertained by a screen.

Impaired Memory & Critical Thinking

- Passive consumption of digital content (such as binge-watching or scrolling) weakens the ability to retain information.
- Kids rely on Google instead of memorizing facts, leading to weaker problem-solving skills and poor critical thinking.

The result? A generation of children who are struggling with focus, patience, and deep thinking—critical skills needed for success in school and life.

2. The Behavioral Impact: From Mood Swings to Digital Tantrums

Technology is not just altering children's cognitive development—it's also affecting their behavior, emotional stability, and ability to self-regulate.

The Rise of "Digital Tantrums"

- Many parents notice that when children are asked to turn off a screen, they react with extreme frustration, aggression, or emotional breakdowns.
- This happens because screens provide a constant source of instant gratification, making children less tolerant of boredom or delayed rewards.

Increased Anxiety & Depression

- Social media introduces children to comparison culture, online validation, and cyberbullying, leading to low self-esteem, anxiety, and depression.
- The fear of missing out (FOMO) and pressure to perform online cause emotional distress in young users.

Sleep Disruptions & Fatigue

- The blue light from screens suppresses melatonin production, making it harder for kids to fall asleep.
- Late-night screen use leads to chronic sleep deprivation, affecting mood, memory, and academic performance.

The Addiction Cycle: Why Kids Keep Craving More

- Just like adults, children experience dopamine-driven screen addiction, making it difficult to stop using digital devices.

- Many apps and games use reward systems, points, and streaks to keep kids engaged for as long as possible.

Bottom line: *The more time children spend on screens, the more they crave them—creating a dependency that affects their mood, behavior, and mental well-being.*

3. Screen Time & Learning: Are Screens Helping or Hurting Education?

With the rise of digital learning tools, many believe that technology enhances education. While this is true in some cases, excessive screen exposure can also hinder academic performance.

The Downside of Digital Learning

- **Reduced Retention**: Information absorbed through screens is often processed passively, leading to weaker memory retention compared to reading physical books or writing notes.
- **Lower Reading Comprehension**: Kids who read on screens tend to skim instead of deeply processing content, leading to weaker comprehension skills.
- **Increased Distractions**: Online learning platforms often have built-in distractions (ads, notifications, other apps), making it harder for kids to stay focused on lessons.

The Power of Hands-On, Real-World Learning

- Tactile activities (writing, drawing, and building) strengthen motor skills and cognitive abilities.
- Outdoor play and physical movement enhance creativity, problem-solving, and emotional resilience.
- Face-to-face learning with teachers and peers builds social intelligence and critical thinking skills that screens cannot replicate.

4. The Road to Recovery: Raising Tech-Smart Kids

Technology is here to stay—but it doesn't have to control childhood. The key is balance, awareness, and mindful use.

Steps to Reduce Screen Dependence in Children

Set Daily Screen Limits

- The American Academy of Pediatrics recommends no more than 1 hour of screen time per day for children under 6 and consistent limits for older kids.

Encourage Outdoor & Offline Activities

- Prioritize sports, creative hobbies, reading, and face-to-face interactions over digital entertainment.

Create Tech-Free Zones & Times

- Keep bedrooms, family meals, and playtime screen-free to encourage real interactions.

Model Healthy Tech Habits as Parents

- Children mimic adults—reduce your own screen time to set a good example.

Use Technology Wisely

- Choose educational apps over entertainment-based content and encourage interactive learning instead of passive consumption.

Encourage Delayed Gratification

- Teach kids to wait and enjoy real-world rewards instead of seeking instant gratification through screens.

Prioritize Sleep Hygiene

- No screens at least 1 hour before bedtime to improve sleep quality and brain function.

Digital Daycare or Consumer Trap? The Dark Truth About YouTube for Kids

Many parents have unknowingly surrendered their children to an invisible empire of manipulation. With just a tap, toddlers are handed over to YouTube, the modern babysitter, while parents revel in a few moments of peace—scrolling social media or finishing chores—completely oblivious to what their little ones are consuming. But this is no harmless cartoon marathon. It's a well-oiled machine of psychological conditioning, turning innocent eyes into lifelong consumers and rewiring young brains for maximum profitability.

Let's be brutally honest: this isn't about entertainment. This is about **control**, **addiction**, and a **ruthless business strategy** that sees your child not as a viewer, but as a revenue source.

YouTube channels aimed at children are not created out of love for kids. They're designed with cold, calculated precision to hijack your child's brain.

The bright visuals, the exaggerated sounds, the endless repetition—it's not accidental. These elements are fine-tuned to keep children's eyes glued to the screen. Animations are made hyperactive, voices are pitched unnaturally high, and scenes shift rapidly to cater to short attention spans. The goal is simple: keep them watching, keep them wanting, keep them consuming.

Beneath the flashing lights and silly songs lies a **predatory business model**. The unboxing videos your child loves? They're not innocent fun.

They're marketing tools—commercials dressed in costume—designed to plant desire. The wide-eyed reactions, the exaggerated excitement, the constant flood of new toys—it's all scripted to make your child believe happiness comes in plastic packaging. And the worst part? Many of these content creators are children themselves, used as puppets by their own parents to sell dreams to other kids.

Yes, it's children selling to children, orchestrated by adults chasing YouTube millions.

But the manipulation doesn't stop at toys. Food branding, clothing lines, and even lifestyle choices are being embedded into videos. Junk food and sugary snacks are casually promoted, often under the radar of advertising regulations, leading kids to crave—and nag—for the same at home.

A child cannot distinguish content from advertising, and that's exactly what marketers exploit. They don't need your approval; they already have your child's trust.

If you're handing your kid a screen just to "get them out of your hair," ask yourself: **Are you raising a child or building a customer base for global brands?** You may believe you're offering them education or entertainment, but in reality, you're offering their attention span, emotional vulnerability, and innocence on a silver platter to corporations that couldn't care less about your child's well-being.

Even more disturbing is the **illusion of safety**. Just because the video has cartoons and a cheerful thumbnail doesn't mean it's harmless. Many "family-friendly" creators sneak in consumerism under the guise of wholesome content. It's manipulation with a smile—and most parents are too distracted or lazy to notice. If you're among those who think "they're just watching harmless videos," perhaps it's time to rewatch them yourself—with open eyes.

Let's talk about the consequences. The constant overstimulation from such content has been linked to attention disorders, sleep disruption, and emotional dysregulation. Harvard Medical School warns that excessive screen exposure during early development can severely impact a child's ability to focus and manage emotions. A study published by Harvard Health states:

"Increased screen time in toddlers and children is associated with delayed development, attention problems, and mood instability.

Still think it's no big deal?

This is a digital jungle where your child is the prey and you're the gatekeeper—yet most parents have thrown away the key. It's easier to hand over the tablet than to set boundaries. Easier to stay ignorant than to monitor. But the cost of that comfort is your child's mental, emotional, and physical health.

So the next time you pass your child a phone with YouTube open, don't fool yourself into thinking it's harmless. You're not just giving them entertainment. You're giving away their attention, their innocence, and their future to an industry that thrives on ignorance and inaction.

It's time to wake up. Not just for your child's sake, but for the society we're shaping—one overstimulated, emotionally blunted, screen-addicted generation at a time.

Learning: Protecting Childhood in the Digital Age

The question is no longer whether technology should be part of children's lives—it already is. The real question is: How do we ensure it enhances childhood rather than replaces it?

If we allow screens to dominate childhood, we risk raising a generation disconnected from reality, emotionally fragile, and unable to focus on deep thinking. But by setting boundaries and promoting healthy tech habits, we can help children grow into thoughtful, creative, and well-rounded individuals— ***not digital zombies.***

Are you ready to take back control? In the next chapter, we will explore actionable digital detox strategies to help families reclaim their time, attention, and mental well-being.

THE TEENAGE DIGITAL DILEMMA

Social Validation, Cyberbullying, and Mental Health Concerns

> *"We are not just addicted to our phones. We are addicted to the validation they provide."*
>
> – **Anonymous**

Teenagers today live in two worlds: the real one and the digital one. While the real world consists of family, school, and physical interactions, the digital world is made up of Instagram posts, Snapchat streaks, TikTok trends, and WhatsApp groups. For many teens, social media is no longer just a tool—it has become a major part of their identity.

But what happens when the need for validation from likes and comments becomes overwhelming? When does cyberbullying replace face-to-face teasing? When mental health struggles intensify due to screen overuse?

This chapter dives deep into the challenges teenagers face in the digital age—the pressure to be "liked," the rise of cyberbullying, and the alarming impact of excessive screen time on mental well-being. More importantly, it provides solutions to help teens navigate these challenges and create a healthier relationship with technology.

1. The Social Validation Trap: Why Teens Crave Online Approval

Teenagers have always sought validation from their peers. In the past, this happened through school interactions, friendships, and achievements. But now, social media has taken over as the primary source of validation.

Why is social media So Addictive for Teens?

- Likes and comments = self-worth: Many teens measure their popularity and self-esteem based on engagement on their posts.
- Fear of Missing Out (FOMO): Seeing others enjoying events, vacations, or achievements online can make a teen feel left out or inadequate.
- Comparison Culture: Social media portrays an unrealistic, filtered version of reality, leading to self-doubt and body image issues.

- Streaks and online friendships: Apps like Snapchat encourage constant communication to maintain "streaks," creating anxiety when they're broken.

The Psychological Toll of Social Validation:

- Anxiety about how many likes a post gets.
- Depression when a friend doesn't comment or reply quickly.
- Self-esteem issues from comparing real life to someone's edited highlight reel.

Reality Check: social media *creates an illusion—it isn't real life. The people who appear perfect online struggle with the same insecurities offline. Learning to detach self-worth from digital validation is crucial for mental well-being.*

2. Cyberbullying: The Silent Epidemic in the Digital Age

Cyberbullying is one of the biggest threats to teenagers' mental health today. Unlike traditional bullying, which was limited to schools and physical spaces, cyberbullying follows teens everywhere—on their phones, in their social media feeds, and even in their private messages.

Common Forms of Cyberbullying:

- **Public Humiliation**: Sharing embarrassing photos or videos to shame someone.
- **Harassment & Threats**: Sending hateful messages or threats online.
- **Fake Profiles**: Creating fake accounts to spread rumors or impersonate someone.
- **Exclusion**: Deliberately leaving someone out of group chats or online conversations.

- **Cancel Culture**: Publicly attacking someone for a mistake, leading to social isolation.

The Impact on Teen Mental Health:

- Victims of cyberbullying experience higher levels of anxiety, depression, and low self-esteem.
- Some teens avoid school, struggle academically, or withdraw from social interactions due to online bullying.
- In extreme cases, cyberbullying has led to self-harm and suicidal thoughts.

How to Combat Cyberbullying

Speak Up: If you're being bullied, talk to a trusted friend, parent, or teacher. Silence allows bullies to continue.

Block & Report: Most social media platforms have tools to block and report abusive users.

Be Kind Online: If you wouldn't say it in person, don't say it online.

Educate & Raise Awareness: Schools, parents, and communities must address cyberbullying openly.

3. The Hidden Mental Health Crisis Among Teens

There has been a dramatic increase in teenage anxiety, depression, and stress in the past decade, and experts believe digital overuse is a major factor.

The Negative Effects of Social Media on Teen Mental Health:

Sleep Deprivation:

- Many teens stay up late scrolling through social media, disrupting sleep patterns.
- Lack of sleep leads to mood swings, lack of focus, and increased stress.

Increased Anxiety & Depression:

- The constant need for validation leads to self-doubt, stress, and low self-worth.
- Studies show that teens who spend more than 3 hours a day on social media have a higher risk of depression.

Addiction & Impulse Control Issues:

- Teens feel anxious without their phones, constantly checking notifications.
- Dopamine-driven addiction makes it harder to focus on schoolwork or real-life activities.

Reduced Face-to-Face Interaction:

- Excessive screen time weakens real-life social skills, making teens more isolated.
- Many prefer texting over real conversations, reducing emotional connections.

The Digital Puppet Masters – Unveiling the Dark Strategies of Gaming Companies

Where pixels dance and virtual worlds beckon, lays a meticulously crafted trap. This isn't just about entertainment; it's about control, manipulation, and profit. Behind every engaging game and enticing notification is a calculated move by gaming companies to capture your attention, alter your behavior, and monetize your time.

The Mechanics of Manipulation

Modern games are no longer simple pastimes; they've evolved into complex systems designed to exploit human psychology:

- **Variable Reward Systems**: Games employ unpredictable reward schedules, akin to slot machines, to keep players engaged. The uncertainty of rewards triggers dopamine release, reinforcing the gaming behavior.
- **Artificial Scarcity**: Limited-time events and exclusive items create a sense of urgency, compelling players to engage more frequently to avoid missing out.
- **Social Pressures**: Multiplayer games often incorporate social elements, where peer pressure and the desire for social acceptance drive prolonged engagement.
- **Microtransactions and Loot Boxes**: These in-game purchases, often randomized, encourage players to spend real money for virtual rewards, blurring the lines between gaming and gambling.

Psychological Warfare: Targeting the Vulnerable

Gaming companies invest heavily in understanding human behavior to make their products more addictive:

- **Exploiting Cognitive Biases**: By leveraging biases like the "sunk cost fallacy," players are encouraged to continue investing time and money to justify previous expenditures.
- **Triggering Emotional Responses**: Games are designed to evoke strong emotions—excitement, frustration, achievement—which reinforce the gaming loop.
- **Creating Dependency**: The integration of daily rewards and streaks fosters habitual behavior, making it challenging for players to disengage.

Real-World Consequences: Beyond the Screen

The impact of these manipulative strategies extends far beyond virtual realms:

- **Mental Health Decline**: Excessive gaming has been linked to increased rates of depression, anxiety, and social isolation among adolescents.
- **Academic and Occupational Impairment**: Time spent gaming often comes at the expense of academic performance and skill development, affecting future career prospects.
- **Financial Strain**: Microtransactions can lead to significant financial losses, especially among youths who may not fully grasp the value of money.
- **Physical Health Issues**: According to the article from the National Library of Medicine (US) Sedentary, lifestyles associated with prolonged gaming contribute to obesity, sleep disturbances, and other health problems.

The Illusion of Control: Are You Playing the Game, or Is It Playing You?

It's crucial to recognize that the sense of control in gaming is often an illusion:

- **Algorithmic Manipulation**: Game algorithms adapt to player behavior, adjusting difficulty and rewards to maintain engagement.
- **Data Exploitation**: Personal data is collected and analyzed to tailor experiences that maximize time spent in-game, often without explicit consent.
- **Normalization of Gambling**: The incorporation of gambling-like elements in games normalizes such behaviors, potentially leading to gambling addictions.

Remember, while games can offer entertainment and even educational value, it's essential to remain vigilant about their potential to manipulate and harm. By staying informed and setting personal boundaries, you can enjoy gaming responsibly without falling into the traps laid by those who prioritize profit over well-being.

How Teens Can Take Control: Practical Solutions

While social media and technology aren't inherently bad, they need to be used in a way that enhances life rather than controls it.

1. Limit Screen Time & Set Boundaries

- Use social media in moderation—don't let it dictate your mood.
- Set a time limit for daily screen use and take breaks.
- Avoid social media at least an hour before bedtime to improve sleep quality.

2. **Detox from Digital Validation**
    - Remind yourself that likes and followers do not define self-worth.
    - Unfollow accounts that make you feel insecure or unhappy.
    - Follow pages that inspire and promote positive mental health.

3. **Focus on Real-Life Relationships**
    - Prioritize face-to-face conversations over texting.
    - Spend quality time with family and real friends.
    - Engage in offline activities—sports, hobbies, and reading.

4. **Be Mindful of What You Post & Consume**
    - Avoid oversharing personal information online.
    - Think before you comment—words can have a lasting impact.
    - Follow content that is educational, uplifting, and inspiring.

5. **Seek Help When Needed**
    - If social media is making you anxious or depressed, talk to someone.
    - Therapy and counseling can help build self-esteem and resilience.
    - Mental health is just as important as physical health—never be afraid to ask for support.

Learning: The Power to Choose

Teenagers today face unprecedented digital challenges, but they also have the power to take control of their digital lives. Social media, online games should be a tool for learning, creativity, and connection—not a source of stress, anxiety, or addiction.

So, ask yourself:

Does social media make you feel better or worse about yourself?

Are You Playing the Game, or Is It Playing You?

If social media and screen time are affecting your mental well-being, take a step back. Prioritize real-life experiences, self-growth, and mental health over digital validation.

In the next chapter, we will explore powerful digital detox strategies that can help you reset your mind, reclaim your time, and build a healthier relationship with technology. Are you ready to take control?

ADULTS & DIGITAL BURNOUT

Productivity Loss, Stress, and How Digital Addiction Ruins Personal and Professional Life

> *"The price of anything is the amount of life you exchange for it."*
> **– Henry David Thoreau**

The modern world demands constant digital engagement. Work emails, social media notifications, endless WhatsApp messages, and the pressure to stay "updated" create a never-ending cycle of digital exhaustion. Many adults wake up and check their phones before even getting out of bed, spend their work hours buried in screens, and wind down at night by binge-watching content—only to feel mentally drained and unfulfilled.

This always-connected lifestyle is leading to a growing crisis: digital burnout. Productivity is declining, stress levels are raising, and personal relationships are suffering. Despite spending most of their waking hours in front of screens, many people feel more disconnected than ever—from themselves, their families, and their passions.

This chapter explores how digital addiction is harming adults, both personally and professionally. More importantly, it provides strategies to break free from digital burnout and regain control over time, energy, and mental well-being.

1. The Illusion of Productivity: How Screens Steal Our Focus

Many adults believe that being online and constantly available makes them more productive. In reality, the opposite is true.

Why Excessive Screen Time Hurts Productivity:

The Multitasking Myth:

- Constantly switching between emails, Slack messages, and social media destroys deep focus.
- Studies show that multitasking reduces productivity by up to 40% because the brain takes time to refocus after each distraction.

The Dopamine Distraction Loop:

- Every notification, like, or email gives a small dopamine rush, making it harder to focus on long-term tasks.
- This creates a habit of checking the phone every few minutes, reducing efficiency.

Information Overload:

- Endless news feeds, online meetings, and group chats create mental clutter, making it hard to prioritize what truly matters.
- Many professionals suffer from decision fatigue, struggling to filter out unnecessary information.

Reality Check: *More screen time doesn't mean more productivity. True efficiency comes from focused, distraction-free work and intentional technology use.*

2. Digital Stress & Anxiety: The Cost of Always Being Online

The always-on culture has blurred the lines between work and personal life. Employees are expected to answer emails after hours, respond to WhatsApp messages instantly, and be available on multiple digital platforms at all times. This constant digital pressure leads to chronic stress and burnout.

Signs of Digital Burnout:

- Feeling exhausted, even after a full night's sleep.
- Increased irritability and frustration, especially with digital interruptions.
- Difficulty concentrating for long periods.
- Lack of motivation or passion for work and personal projects.

- Physical symptoms like headaches, eye strain, and poor posture from excessive screen use.

The Long-Term Impact of Digital Stress:

- Higher risk of anxiety, depression, and emotional exhaustion.
- Increased risk of cardiovascular diseases due to chronic stress.
- Reduced creativity and problem-solving skills due to constant digital stimulation.

Solution: Create boundaries—separate work from personal time, limit notifications, and take intentional breaks from screens.

3. The Digital Addiction That Ruins Personal Life

It's not just work that keeps adults glued to screens. Digital addiction extends into personal time, often at the cost of relationships and real-world experiences.

How Digital Overuse Affects Personal Life:

Relationships Suffer:

- Many couples spend more time scrolling through social media than having meaningful conversations.
- Parents are distracted by their phones, missing out on quality time with children.

Emotional Numbness & Loneliness:

- Social media and binge-watching create an illusion of connection, but in reality, many feel lonelier than ever.
- Excessive screen use leads to reduced emotional intelligence and weaker interpersonal skills.

Poor Physical Health:

- Less movement leads to obesity, poor posture, and chronic health issues.
- Screen-induced insomnia disrupts sleep patterns, leading to fatigue and mood swings.

The Wake-Up Call: If digital habits are damaging relationships, mental health, and well-being, it's time to reassess priorities and set limits.

4. How to Break Free: Practical Solutions for Digital Detox

1. Set Digital Boundaries

- Define "no-screen zones" at home (e.g., bedrooms, dining tables).
- Turn off work notifications after office hours to maintain work-life balance.

2. Control Your Screen Time

- Use apps like Forest, Freedom, or Focus Mode to block distractions.
- Limit social media use to 30-60 minutes per day for better mental health.

3. Prioritize Deep Work & Real-Life Activities

- Follow the Pomodoro technique: Work deeply for 25–50 minutes, then take a 5-minute break.
- Spend at least 1 hour a day on hobbies or family time without screens.

4. Unplug Before Bed

- Stop screen use at least 1 hour before bedtime to improve sleep.
- Read a book, meditate, or listen to calming music instead.

5. **Digital Detox Days**

- Take one full day per week with minimal or no screen time.
- Engage in outdoor activities, family bonding, or creative projects.

Learning: Regaining Control of Life

Digital technology is a powerful tool, but when overused, it takes away more than it gives. Many adults are trapped in a cycle of digital burnout—working harder but achieving less, staying connected yet feeling isolated.

But there is a way out. By setting boundaries, prioritizing real-life experiences, and practicing mindful technology use, it's possible to reclaim time, energy, and mental clarity.

The question is: Are you in control of your digital habits, or are they controlling you?

In the next chapter, we'll explore the ultimate digital detox strategies—a step-by-step guide to breaking free from digital addiction and building a balanced, fulfilling life. Are you ready to unplug and reclaim your focus?

THE PHYSICAL TOLL OF DIGITAL OVERUSE

Eye Strain, Sleep Disorders, and Posture-Related Health Issues

> *"Take care of your body. It's the only place you have to live."*
>
> **– Jim Rohn**

Screens are everywhere. From the moment we wake up to the time we sleep, our eyes, hands, and posture are constantly engaged with digital devices. Whether it's smartphones, laptops, tablets, or televisions, the human body is paying a heavy price for excessive screen time.

While the mental and emotional effects of digital addiction are widely discussed, its physical consequences are often overlooked. The reality is that excessive digital use is reshaping our bodies in damaging ways, leading to chronic eye strain, disrupted sleep cycles, posture-related health problems, and even long-term musculoskeletal disorders.

This chapter explores the physical toll of digital overuse, explaining how screens affect our eyes, sleep, spine, and overall well-being. More importantly, it provides practical solutions to counteract these effects and build healthier habits.

1. Digital Eye Strain: The Price of Constant Screen Use

Do you experience:

Blurry vision after long screen sessions?
Dry, irritated eyes?
Frequent headaches?
Sensitivity to light?

If so, you may be suffering from Digital Eye Strain (DES), also known as Computer Vision Syndrome (CVS)—a condition caused by prolonged exposure to digital screens.

Why Screens Harm the Eyes:

Blue Light Exposure: Digital screens emit high-energy blue light, which penetrates deeper into the eyes than natural light, causing strain and fatigue.

Reduced Blinking: While reading or watching on screens, we blink 50% less, leading to dryness, irritation, and discomfort.

Constant Refocusing: Unlike printed text, digital screens require the eyes to constantly adjust focus, leading to fatigue.

How to Protect Your Eyes:

Follow the 20-20-20 Rule: Every 20 minutes, look 20 feet away for 20 seconds to relax your eye muscles.

Adjust Screen Brightness: Keep screens at a comfortable brightness level. Avoid using screens in complete darkness.

Use Blue Light Filters: Enable night mode or blue light blocking glasses to reduce eye strain.

Artificial Tears: Use lubricating eye drops if your eyes feel dry or irritated.

2. Sleep Disorders: The Hidden Danger of Nighttime Screen Use

Do you struggle with:

Difficulty falling asleep?

Waking up feeling tired?

Restless sleep patterns?

If yes, your screen habits may be disrupting your sleep cycle. Studies show that excessive screen time before bed reduces sleep quality, making people feel tired even after 7-8 hours of sleep.

Why Screens Disrupt Sleep:

Blue Light Suppresses Melatonin:

- Melatonin is the hormone that tells the body it's time to sleep.
- Blue light from screens blocks melatonin production, keeping the brain awake longer.

Overstimulation Before Bed:

- Watching intense content (social media, news, Netflix) keeps the brain hyperactive, making it hard to relax.

Midnight Scrolling & Doomscrolling:

- Many people check their phones in bed, delaying sleep and disrupting deep sleep cycles.

How to Improve Sleep:

No Screens 1 Hour Before Bed: Replace screen time with reading, meditation, or soft music.

Use Night Mode: If screen use is necessary, enable warm light settings to reduce blue light.

Create a Bedtime Routine: Set a fixed sleeping schedule and stick to it.

Keep Devices Out of the Bedroom: Charge phones away from the bed to avoid temptation.

3. Posture Problems & "Tech Neck": How Screens Are Destroying Our Spine

Common Digital Posture Issues:

Tech Neck (Text Neck): Stiff neck and shoulder pain from looking down at screens.

Hunched Back (Kyphosis): Rounded shoulders and bad posture from prolonged sitting. **Wrist & Finger Pain (Repetitive Strain Injury):** Pain from excessive typing and scrolling.

Lower Back Pain: Sitting for long hours weakens the spine, leading to chronic back pain.

How Screens Damage Posture:

Forward Head Position (Tech Neck):

- The human head weighs around 10-12 pounds.
- Looking down at a phone increases the pressure on the neck up to 60 pounds, causing strain and pain.

Sitting Too Long Weakens the Spine:

- Extended sitting reduces blood flow and stiffens muscles.
- Over time, this leads to chronic back pain, poor posture, and even nerve damage.

How to Improve Posture & Reduce Pain:

Maintain Proper Screen Height: Keep screens at eye level to reduce neck strain.

Take Frequent Breaks: Stand up and stretch every 30-60 minutes.

Use Ergonomic Chairs & Desks: Support the spine with a good chair and proper desk height.

Stretch & Exercise: Perform posture correction exercises like neck rolls, shoulder shrugs, and back stretches.

4. The Long-Term Health Risks of Digital Overuse

Excessive screen time doesn't just cause temporary discomfort—it can lead to serious, long-term health problems.

The Hidden Health Risks:

Obesity & Heart Disease – Sitting too much slows metabolism, increasing the risk of weight gain, diabetes, and heart problems.

Chronic Pain & Arthritis – Poor posture and repetitive hand movements can cause permanent joint issues.

Increased Risk of Stroke & Blood Clots – Prolonged sitting reduces circulation, increasing the risk of blood clots.

How to Reverse the Damage:

Stay Active – Walk, stretch, or exercise daily to counteract the effects of sitting.

Limit Unnecessary Screen Time – Reduce non-essential scrolling and binge-watching.

Follow Healthy Digital Habits – Use ergonomic workspaces, take breaks, and maintain good posture.

Learning: Taking Control of Your Health

Technology is an incredible tool, but our bodies were not designed for endless screen exposure. Ignoring the physical effects of digital overuse can lead to chronic pain, poor health, and long-term damage.

The good news? It's never too late to make a change. By adopting simple habits like adjusting screen time, improving posture, and prioritizing sleep, you can protect your body and improve overall well-being.

The question is: Are you ready to take control of your health before screens take control of you?

In the next chapter, we'll explore practical steps to build a healthy, balanced digital lifestyle—without sacrificing productivity or entertainment.

FAMILY & RELATIONSHIPS IN THE DIGITAL AGE

How Excessive Screen Time is Affecting Personal Bonds

> *"The greatest gift you can give someone is your time. Because when you give your time, you are giving a portion of your life that you will never get back."*
>
> **– Rick Warren**

In an era where people are more connected than ever, we have ironically never been more disconnected from the people who matter most—our family and loved ones. Dinner tables have become silent as screens take center stage. Conversations are interrupted by notifications. Children are growing up in homes where parents are physically present but mentally absent.

The digital age has reshaped the way families interact, often replacing face-to-face conversations with texts, emojis, and social media updates. While technology can help families stay connected across distances, excessive screen time is eroding the quality of relationships at home, creating emotional distance, misunderstandings, and even resentment among loved ones.

This chapter explores how the overuse of digital devices is affecting parent-child relationships, marriages, friendships, and overall family dynamics, and offers practical steps to rebuild meaningful, in-person connections in a hyper-digital world.

1. The Silent Killer of Relationships: Digital Distraction

The Reality of Tech-Driven Disconnection

- Parents who are scrolling on their phones while their kids seek attention.
- Couples sitting together yet lost in separate digital worlds.
- Teenagers who are glued to their screens, preferring virtual chats over real conversations.
- Families watching TV together—but not actually talking to each other.

The rise of "phubbing" (phone snubbing)—ignoring someone in favor of a smartphone—has become a relationship killer. Studies show that partners who frequently experience "phubbing" feel less satisfied in their relationships, leading to emotional distance and communication breakdowns.

The Harsh Truth:

We spend more time with screens than with our loved ones.
We reply to messages faster than we respond to people sitting next to us.
We are "connected" to the world but disconnected from our family.

Reflection: When was the last time you had a deep, uninterrupted conversation with your family without checking your phone?

2. The Impact of Screen Time on Parent-Child Relationships

The "Distracted Parent Syndrome"

Today's children are growing up with "digitally absent" parents—mothers and fathers who are physically present but constantly distracted by their devices.

Effects of Parental Digital Distraction:

Children feel neglected and unimportant when parents prioritize their phones over them.

Lack of emotional connection can lead to behavioral issues, low self-esteem, and attention-seeking behaviors.

Screen habits are passed down—kids mirror their parents' screen addiction, leading to early tech dependency.

The Harsh Reality:

A study found that toddlers misbehave more when parents use their phones excessively because they feel emotionally ignored. Another report shows that 60% of children believe their parents spend too much time on screens.

Solution:

Implement "No-Phone Zones" during meals, family outings, and bedtime.

Practice "Screen-Free Eye Contact"—give full attention when speaking to your child.

Schedule "Tech-Free Family Time"—a set period where everyone unplugs and engages in real interactions.

THE CORPORATE & WORKPLACE DIGITAL ADDICTION

How Work-Related Digital Overload is Impacting Efficiency and Mental Well-Being

> *"To perform one's duty with sincerity and dedication, without attachment to the results, is the highest form of worship."*
>
> – **Bhagavad Gita**

The modern workplace has become a battlefield of endless emails, constant notifications, and digital distractions. Employees are always "on," expected to respond instantly, multitask relentlessly, and remain connected even after office hours. This has led to a new form of workplace epidemic: digital addiction at work.

While technology was supposed to make work easier, it has instead created overload, burnout, and reduced productivity. The lines between professional and personal life have blurred, making it difficult for employees to disconnect and recharge.

In this chapter, we explore how workplace digital addiction is impacting employees' efficiency, mental health, and overall well-being, and discuss strategies to regain balance in an era of hyperconnectivity.

1. The Illusion of Productivity: Are We Really Getting More Done?

The Modern Workplace Reality:

- Employees check their email every 6 minutes on average.
- Most workers spend at least 3 hours per day just managing emails.
- Multitasking reduces productivity by 40%—yet most employees are forced to juggle multiple tasks at once.
- The average worker is interrupted every 11 minutes, but it takes 25 minutes to regain full focus after an interruption.

Many believe that being constantly connected = being productive, but research proves otherwise. Digital overload leads to stress, decision fatigue, and lower-quality work.

Key Insight: True productivity is not about working more hours but working smarter by minimizing distractions.

2. The Email Trap: A Never-Ending To-Do List

Is Email Controlling Your Workday?

For many professionals, the workday begins and ends with checking and responding to emails. But email, instead of being a productivity tool, has become a major source of distraction and stress.

The Problems with Excessive Email Usage:

Constant Interruptions – Every notification shifts your focus away from real work.

Inbox Anxiety – Feeling overwhelmed by an endless flow of unread emails.

False Productivity – Spending hours answering emails instead of working on meaningful tasks.

After-Hours Pressure – Expectation to reply to emails at night or on weekends.

Solution:

Set Fixed Email Hours – Check emails only 2-3 times per day instead of constantly.

Use the "2-Minute Rule" – If an email takes less than 2 minutes to answer, respond immediately; if not, schedule time to handle it later.

Unsubscribe & Filter – Reduce inbox clutter by unsubscribing from unnecessary emails and using filters to prioritize important messages.

3. The Tyranny of Notifications: A Constant Distraction

How Notifications Are Ruining Focus

- The average worker receives 80+ notifications per day from emails, chats, and apps.
- A single notification can reduce focus for up to 15 minutes.
- Frequent interruptions increase stress and lower creativity.

Solution:

Turn Off Non-Essential Notifications – Disable alerts for social media, newsletters, and unimportant apps.

Use "Do Not Disturb" Mode – Block all notifications during deep work sessions.

Batch Check Messages – Instead of reacting to notifications instantly, set fixed times to check them.

4. Zoom Fatigue & Virtual Meeting Overload

Are You Spending More Time in Meetings Than Doing Actual Work?

With remote work becoming the norm, Zoom meetings have skyrocketed, but excessive virtual meetings lead to:

Mental exhaustion – Staring at screens for hours drains energy.

Reduced deep work – Constant meetings leave little time for focused tasks.

Camera Anxiety – The pressure to always be visible and engaged is stressful.

Solution:

Reduce Unnecessary Meetings – Not everything needs a meeting; use emails or collaboration tools instead.

Set Meeting-Free Hours – Block time for deep, uninterrupted work.

Encourage Shorter Meetings – Stick to a 30-minute limit whenever possible.

5. The Dark Side of Work-From-Home: The 24/7 Work Trap

Remote Work = More Freedom or More Work?

While working from home offers flexibility, it has also:

Blurred boundaries between work and personal life.

Increased after-hours communication expectations.

Led to higher levels of burnout due to an "always available" culture.

The Solution:

- Set clear work hours and log off completely at the end of the day.
- Create a separate workspace to mentally separate work from home life.
- Communicate boundaries—let your team know when you're offline.

6. Digital Burnout: The Cost of Over-Connectivity

Symptoms of Digital Burnout in the Workplace:

Mental Fatigue – Feeling drained, even after short tasks.

Reduced Focus – Struggling to concentrate due to constant digital overload.

Emotional Detachment – Losing interest in work and feeling disconnected.

Physical Symptoms – Headaches, insomnia, and eye strain from excessive screen time.

The Long-Term Consequences:

- Higher stress levels lead to anxiety and depression.
- Lower job satisfaction reduces motivation and engagement.
- Increased absenteeism due to exhaustion and mental health issues.

How to Prevent Burnout:

Take Regular Breaks – Use the Pomodoro Technique (25 min work, 5 min break) to stay refreshed.

Practice Digital Detox – Step away from screens during lunch breaks and after work.

Incorporate Mindfulness – Meditation, deep breathing, or stretching can help reset your mind.

7. Creating a Healthier Digital Work Culture

How Organizations Can Reduce Digital Overload

- Encourage "Right to Disconnect" Policies – No work emails after office hours.
- Limit Meetings & Emails – Focus on efficiency rather than endless communication.
- Promote Mental Well-Being – Offer digital detox programs and encourage work-life balance.
- Educate Employees on Healthy Tech Use – Provide training on managing screen time effectively.

Learning: Taking Back Control Over Digital Work Life

The workplace should enhance productivity, not drain employees through excessive digital demands. The solution is not to eliminate technology but to use it mindfully—with clear boundaries, structured focus time, and intentional breaks.

Ask Yourself:

Am I working efficiently, or just staying busy with digital distractions?

Do I feel constantly overwhelmed by emails, notifications, and meetings?

What small change can I make today to regain control over my digital work habits?

Work smarter, not harder. Disconnect to reconnect with what truly matters.

PART 2

BREAKING FREE FROM THE DIGITAL CHAINS

11. The Power of Awareness: First Step to Detox – Recognizing and accepting the problem.
12. Mind Over Machine: Rewiring Your Brain – Psychological strategies to break free from compulsive usage.
13. Creating Healthy Digital Boundaries – Practical rules for limiting screen time.
14. Detoxing social media – Managing or eliminating toxic platforms from daily life.
15. Understanding FOMO (Fear of Missing Out) & Digital Anxiety – How to overcome the fear of being disconnected.
16. Breaking Free from Dopamine Loops – How to reset your brain for long-term digital control.
17. Digital Minimalism: Less is More – Using technology with intention, not addiction.
18. Reclaiming Focus & Mental Clarity – How to restore attention span, creativity, and deep thinking.
19. The Art of Mindful Technology Use – Learning to use tech without being controlled by it.
20. How to Handle Peer Pressure & Social Expectations – Resisting digital addiction in a hyper-connected world.

THE POWER OF AWARENESS – THE FIRST STEP TO DETOX

Recognizing and Accepting the Problem

> *"We cannot change what we are not aware of, and once we are aware, we cannot help but change."*
>
> **– Sheryl Sandberg**

Before any transformation can happen, the first and most important step is awareness. We cannot break free from digital addiction if we refuse to recognize its existence in our lives. Many people underestimate the impact of excessive screen time, dismissing it as normal or unavoidable. But the truth is, the habitual overuse of technology is silently taking control of our minds, habits, relationships, and overall well-being.

This chapter is about understanding and acknowledging the problem. It's about looking at our own habits honestly—without denial or excuses—and accepting that change is necessary. Awareness is not about blame or guilt, but about empowerment. Once we see the problem clearly, we take the first step toward regaining control and living with intention rather than mindless scrolling.

1. The Invisible Addiction: Are We Even Aware?

Most people don't realize they are addicted to their screens. Unlike alcohol or drugs, digital addiction is socially accepted, encouraged, and even rewarded.

Common Rationalizations We Tell Ourselves:

"I need my phone for work."
"I can stop anytime I want."
"Everyone spends this much time online."
"I only use social media to stay informed."
"I'm not addicted, I'm just staying connected."

But awareness requires honesty. Instead of excuses, we need to reflect on our habits and ask difficult questions:

- Do I reach for my phone first thing in the morning and last thing before bed?
- Do I feel restless or anxious when my phone is out of reach?

Do I spend more time on screens than with my family or friends?
Have I neglected important tasks, work, or hobbies because of screen time?
Do I feel mentally exhausted, distracted, or overwhelmed due to digital overload?

If you answered "yes" to most of these, then it's time to recognize the issue and take action.

2. Breaking Through Denial: Facing the Truth

Denial keeps us trapped. Many people ignore the signs of digital addiction because it's uncomfortable to admit that something so ordinary—checking our phones, watching videos, scrolling endlessly—could be a serious problem.

Breaking Through Denial Starts with Self-Reflection:

Keep a Screen Time Journal – Track how many hours you spend on devices daily.
Ask Loved Ones for Honest Feedback – Do they feel ignored or neglected because of your screen use?
Observe Your Emotional State – Do you feel drained, irritable, or distracted after long hours on screens?

Awareness Exercise:

For one day, try not to use your phone unless absolutely necessary. Pay attention to how often you reach for it out of habit. How does it feel? Are you more focused? More present? Or do you feel anxious without it?

This simple challenge reveals how deeply screens have infiltrated our daily lives.

3. The Science of Self-Awareness: Why It Matters

Self-awareness is the foundation of any meaningful change. Without it, we remain stuck in habits that damage our productivity, relationships, and mental health.

Research Shows:

People underestimate their screen time by an average of 50%!

The brain automates digital behaviors, making them feel natural—even when they are harmful.

The more aware we are of our habits, the more likely we are to change them.

The Good News?

Once we become aware, we can start making small, conscious choices to reduce digital dependency—without feeling deprived or forced.

4. From Awareness to Action: Shifting Mindset

Recognizing the problem is just the first step. The next step is taking ownership.

Mindset Shifts That Lead to Digital Detox:
From "I need my phone" → "I can take breaks and still function perfectly."
From "I don't have time to detox" → "I control my time, not my screen."
From "Everyone does this" → "I choose what's best for me."

Takeaway: You don't have to quit technology, but you can use it mindfully, not mindlessly.

Learning: Acknowledgment = Power

Digital detox is not about rejecting technology—it's about reclaiming control. The moment you become aware of how digital addiction is affecting you; you've already taken the first and most important step toward a healthier, more present life.

Ask Yourself:

Am I truly in control of my screen time, or is it controlling me?
What habits am I willing to change to regain balance?
How will I take the next step toward digital well-being?

The power to change is in your hands. Awareness is the beginning—now, let's take action.

CHAPTER 12

MIND OVER MACHINE – REWIRING YOUR BRAIN

Psychological Strategies to Break Free from Compulsive Usage

> *"The mind is everything. What you think, you become."*
>
> – **Buddha**

In today's digital world, we are constantly bombarded with notifications, infinite scrolls, and dopamine-driven algorithms designed to keep us hooked. The more we engage with screens, the more our brain rewires itself to crave instant gratification, leading to compulsive behaviors. This isn't just a habit—it's a psychological battle between the rational mind and the addictive nature of digital technology.

The good news? Our brains are adaptable. Just as technology has conditioned us into compulsive usage, we can rewire our minds to regain control. This chapter explores powerful psychological strategies to break free from digital addiction, helping you reclaim focus, self-discipline, and peace of mind.

1. Understanding the Brain's Addiction Loop

Why Does Screen Addiction Feel Uncontrollable?

- Every notification, like, or message triggers a dopamine release, the same chemical involved in addiction to gambling or drugs.
- The brain learns to crave quick digital rewards, making real-life tasks feel boring in comparison.
- Social media and apps exploit psychological vulnerabilities—like the fear of missing out (FOMO) and the need for validation.
- Over time, we develop automatic behaviors, where we instinctively check our phones without thinking.

The Key Insight? The more we reinforce compulsive screen habits, the harder they become to break. But we can reprogram our minds to resist digital temptations.

2. The Power of Self-Discipline: Reclaiming Control

The 5-Second Rule (Mel Robbins)

If you feel the urge to check your phone, count backward from 5, then redirect your attention to something productive. This interrupts automatic behavior patterns and gives your rational brain time to take control.

The Delay Gratification Technique

Instead of reaching for your phone immediately, set a timer for 10 minutes. If the urge disappears before the time is up, you've successfully resisted the impulse. Over time, this reduces compulsive habits.

Create Friction to Reduce Usage

- Remove addictive apps from your home screen.
- Use grayscale mode (less visually stimulating).
- Log out of social media after each session.
- Turn off notifications to reduce external triggers.

The Goal? Make it harder to engage in mindless screen use.

3. Mindfulness: Training the Brain for Digital Discipline

Mindfulness is one of the most powerful tools for breaking compulsive behaviors. It helps us observe urges without acting on them, reducing mindless scrolling and endless distractions.
Mindfulness Strategies to Reduce Digital Dependence:

"Pause Before You Swipe" – Before opening an app, take a deep breath and ask: *Do I really need to do this?*

Use a 3-Minute Meditation App – Instead of checking your phone, take 3 deep breaths and focus on the present moment.

Eat, Walk, and Socialize Without Screens – Train your brain to enjoy life without digital stimulation.

Mindfulness shifts your brain from autopilot mode to intentional living.

4. The Digital Detox Mentality: Changing How You View Technology

To break free from screen addiction, we must change our relationship with technology. Instead of seeing screens as entertainment or escape, reframe them as tools for purposeful use.

Mindset Shifts for Digital Freedom:
From Passive Scrolling → Intentional Engagement (*Use social media for learning, not mindless entertainment.*)
From Always Available → Setting Boundaries (*Your time is valuable. Protect it from unnecessary digital distractions.*)
From Instant Gratification → Delayed Rewards (*Train your brain to seek long-term fulfillment instead of short bursts of pleasure.*)

5. The 30-Day Digital Reset Challenge

Breaking screen addiction requires consistent effort. A structured detox plan helps the brain rewire itself and build healthier habits.

Week-by-Week Detox Strategy:

Week 1: Awareness & Tracking – Monitor screen time and identify addictive patterns.
Week 2: Reduce Digital Temptations – Remove unnecessary apps, disable notifications, and set phone-free zones.

Week 3: Replace Digital Habits – Replace mindless scrolling with reading, exercise, or hobbies.
Week 4: Full Digital Reset – Take a 24-hour no-phone challenge to experience true freedom.

The Goal? Teach your brain to function without digital dependence.

Learning: Take Control, Reclaim Your Mind

The Key to Digital Freedom?

- Awareness of your screen habits.
- Self-discipline to resist compulsive urges.
- Mindfulness to stay present in the real world.
- Intentional technology uses instead of mindless consumption.

Ask Yourself:

- Am I using technology as a tool, or is it using me?
- What psychological strategies will help me break free?
- How can I start rewiring my brain today?

The power is in your hands. Choose your mind over the machine.

CREATING HEALTHY DIGITAL BOUNDARIES

Practical Rules for Limiting Screen Time

> *"You can't do big things if you're distracted by small things."*
>
> **– Robin Sharma**

In the age of constant connectivity, our screens demand our attention 24/7. Work emails, social media updates, breaking news alerts, and endless notifications keep us trapped in a cycle of digital dependency. Without clear boundaries, technology can easily invade our personal time, relationships, sleep, and mental well-being.

But here's the truth: technology isn't the problem—our lack of boundaries is. Learning to set and enforce healthy digital limits is key to breaking free from compulsive usage. In this chapter, we will explore practical strategies to establish balance, regain control over our time, and use technology with intention rather than impulse.

1. Why Digital Boundaries Matter

- Without boundaries, screens control us instead of the other way around.
- Too much screen time leads to stress, anxiety, and poor focus.
- Uncontrolled digital use disrupts relationships, work-life balance, and sleep.
- Boundaries help us protect our time and energy for what truly matters.

The Key Insight?

Just as we set boundaries in relationships and work schedules, we must also set boundaries with technology to maintain a healthy, balanced life.

2. The Golden Rules of Digital Boundaries

Rule #1: No Screens in the First and Last Hour of the Day

Why? Checking your phone first thing in the morning spikes stress levels and reduces productivity. At night, screen exposure disrupts melatonin production, leading to poor sleep.

Solution: Start your day with meditation, reading, or exercise. At night, create a tech-free bedtime routine.

Rule #2: Create "Tech-Free Zones" at Home

Why? Constant device usage erodes family time and real-life interactions.

Solution: Designate areas like the dining table, bedroom, and family room as screen-free zones.

Rule #3: Set Screen Time Limits for social media & Entertainment

Why? Apps are designed for endless engagement, making it easy to lose hours mindlessly scrolling.

Solution: Use screen time tracking apps to set daily limits (e.g., 30 minutes on social media per day).

Rule #4: Use the "One-Screen Rule"

Why? Multitasking with multiple screens (watching TV while scrolling on the phone) overloads the brain and reduces focus.

Solution: Stick to one screen at a time to stay fully engaged in the present moment.

Rule #5: Set Work & Personal Screen Boundaries

Why? Constant emails and notifications keep the mind always "on," leading to digital burnout.

Solution:

- No work emails after office hours.
- Use "Do Not Disturb" mode after a set time each day.
- Take digital breaks during work to reset focus.

3. How to Enforce Digital Boundaries (Without Feeling Guilty)

- **Start Small** – Choose one or two rules to implement first.
- **Inform Others** – Let colleagues, friends, and family know your digital boundaries.
- **Use Technology to Control Technology** – Apps like Freedom, Forest, and Off time help enforce screen time limits.
- **Replace Digital Habits with Real-Life Activities** – Swap screen time with reading, exercise, hobbies, or outdoor activities.
- **Stay Consistent** – Boundaries work only if enforced regularly.

> Remember: Digital boundaries aren't about restricting technology—they're about protecting your time, relationships, and mental clarity.

Learning: Take Back Control

Technology should work for you, not control you. By setting clear digital boundaries, you can reclaim your time, focus, and mental peace.

Ask Yourself:

- Which screen habits are draining my time and energy?
- What digital boundaries do I need to set for a healthier lifestyle?
- How will I start enforcing them today?

The power is in your hands. Set boundaries, stay mindful, and live with intention.

DETOXING SOCIAL MEDIA

Managing or Eliminating Toxic Platforms from Daily Life

> *"Social media is like junk food for the brain. A little won't hurt, but too much will leave you sick, sluggish, and craving more."*
>
> **– Cal Newport**

Social media started as a way to connect people, share ideas, and stay informed. But over time, it has transformed into a highly addictive, emotionally draining, and often toxic environment. Algorithms are designed to hijack our attention, while endless scrolling keeps us trapped in a cycle of comparison, negativity, and distraction.

Many people recognize the problem but struggle to break free. The key isn't just deleting apps—it's reclaiming control over your digital habits. In this chapter, we'll explore how to detox from social media, manage it more intentionally, or even eliminate it completely to regain mental clarity, productivity, and real-life happiness.

1. Understanding Social Media's Toxic Impact

How social media Hijacks Your Brain:

- **Dopamine Loops** – Likes, comments, and shares trigger dopamine spikes, creating an addictive cycle.
- **Comparison Trap** – Seeing highlight reels of others' lives leads to low self-esteem and dissatisfaction.
- **Negativity & Misinformation** – Online debates, outrage culture, and fake news fuel stress and anxiety.
- **Time Drain** – Hours slip away mindlessly scrolling, leaving little time for real-life goals and relationships.

Key Insight: social media isn't inherently bad, but uncontrolled use turns it into a toxic, time-consuming habit.

2. How to Detox from Social Media

Step 1: Identify Your Social Media Triggers

Ask yourself:

- Why do I use social media? (*Boredom, validation, news, distraction?*)

- How do I feel after scrolling? (*Inspired or drained?*)
- Which platforms add value, and which ones waste my time?

The Goal: Become aware of your usage patterns and recognize what needs to change.

Step 2: Declutter & Unfollow Toxic Content

Decluttering your feed is like decluttering your mind. Remove anything that drains your energy.
Unfollow negative, fake, or time-wasting accounts.
Mute or block sources of toxicity, gossip, and drama.
Follow only valuable, inspiring, and educational content.

The Goal: Create a positive and intentional online space.

Step 3: Set Clear Time Limits

Instead of quitting cold turkey, start by reducing screen time.
Use the 30-Minute Rule – Set a daily time limit for social media.
Remove Social Apps from Your Home Screen – Reduce mindless checking.
Use Screen Time Apps – Tools like Freedom, off time, or Forest help control usage.

The Goal: Train your brain to use social media mindfully, not compulsively.

Step 4: Create No-Social Zones & Times

Designate social-free times and places to break the habit.
No social media during meals or conversations.
No scrolling the first hour after waking up or before bed.
One full "No Social Day" per week (Digital Sabbath).

The Goal: Reclaim your focus and presence in real life.

3. Should You Quit Social Media Completely?

Many people find that reducing social media is enough—but for others, quitting completely leads to greater happiness and productivity.

Signs You Should Quit social media:

It negatively impacts your mental health (anxiety, low self-esteem).
You spend more time scrolling than living your real life.
It's affecting your relationships or work productivity.
You feel addicted and can't control your usage.

The Solution? Try a 30-Day Social Media Detox and see how it impacts your mood, focus, and relationships.

4. Replacing Social Media with Real-Life Fulfillment

Instead of scrolling, try:

Reading books or listening to podcasts.
Engaging in hobbies (music, art, sports).
Journaling, meditating, or spending time outdoors.
Building deeper, face-to-face relationships.

The Goal: Fill your time with activities that bring genuine happiness, not digital distractions.

Learning: Take Back Your Time & Mind

Social media should serve you, not control you. Whether you manage it intentionally or eliminate it completely, the key is to live life on your own terms.

Ask Yourself:

- Does social media add value to my life, or is it draining me?
- How can I reduce toxic digital habits today?
- What real-life activities can replace my scrolling time?

You have the power to break free. Start detoxing today and reclaim your time, focus, and mental well-being!

UNDERSTANDING FOMO & DIGITAL ANXIETY

How to Overcome the Fear of Being Disconnected

> *"We must shift our mindset from FOMO (Fear of Missing Out) to JOMO (Joy of Missing Out)."*
>
> **– Arianna Huffington**

The modern digital world thrives on constant updates, notifications, and the illusion of being "always in the loop." Social media, news feeds, and messaging apps create a pressure to stay connected, informed, and engaged at all times. This fear of missing something important—whether it's a social event, a viral trend, or breaking news—is called FOMO (Fear of Missing Out).

While staying informed seems harmless, FOMO leads to digital anxiety, stress, and an unhealthy dependence on technology. Many people feel uneasy when they disconnect from their phones, fearing they'll miss a message, an invitation, or a trending conversation. But here's the truth: staying plugged in all the time is neither necessary nor healthy. In this chapter, we'll explore how to identify and overcome digital anxiety, embrace JOMO (Joy of Missing Out), and break free from the fear of disconnection.

1. What is FOMO? Why Does It Happen?

FOMO is the fear that something important is happening without you. It makes you feel:

Compelled to check social media constantly to stay updated.
Anxious when you see others enjoying experiences you're not part of.
Worried that disconnecting means you'll miss out on opportunities or information.
Mentally drained from trying to keep up with everything.

Why Does FOMO Happen?

- **Social Media Illusions** – People post only their best moments, creating a false sense that life is always exciting.
- **Endless Updates** – News cycles, trends, and notifications keep us in a state of urgency.

- **Comparison Culture** – Seeing others' achievements or outings can trigger self-doubt and dissatisfaction.
- **Brain Chemistry** – Dopamine hits from likes, messages, and updates make digital engagement feel rewarding but addictive.

Key Insight: FOMO isn't about missing out—it's about feeling like what you have isn't enough.

2. The Link Between FOMO & Digital Anxiety

- Constant connectivity leads to stress and exhaustion.
- Doomscrolling increases fear, negativity, and uncertainty.
- Pressure to keep up leads to sleep problems and mental burnout.
- Social comparison causes low self-worth and dissatisfaction.

The Real Problem? FOMO doesn't let you live in the present because you're always worried about what's happening elsewhere.

The Shift You Need? Move from FOMO to JOMO – The Joy of Missing Out!

3. How to Overcome FOMO & Embrace JOMO

Step 1: Recognize FOMO When It Strikes

Pause and ask yourself:
Am I checking my phone out of habit or real need?
Do I actually want to engage, or do I feel pressured?
Is this making me feel good, or am I feeling anxious?

- Awareness is the first step to breaking free from FOMO.

Step 2: Limit Social Media & Digital Noise

Turn Off Notifications – Disable non-essential alerts to reduce distractions.

Schedule social media Time – Instead of checking all day, limit usage to 30 minutes or specific time slots.
Unfollow Accounts That Trigger FOMO – Remove influencers or pages that make you feel inadequate.
Take Social Media Breaks – Try a digital detox weekend to reset your mind.

The Goal? Control your digital habits instead of letting them control you.

Step 3: Shift Focus from Virtual to Real-Life Experiences

Instead of scrolling, engage in real-life activities that bring joy:
Spend time with family and friends without distractions.
Develop a new hobby or creative passion.
Enjoy nature and physical activities instead of digital consumption.
Read books, write, or practice mindfulness.

The Key Insight? Real joy comes from meaningful, offline experiences—not digital updates.

Step 4: Rewire Your Mindset – Embrace JOMO

What if missing out was actually a good thing?
JOMO (Joy of Missing Out) means choosing peace over pressure.
It's about appreciating the present rather than worrying about the virtual world.
It's the freedom to disconnect without guilt.

How to Embrace JOMO?

- Reframe Disconnection as Self-Care – Missing out on digital noise gives you mental clarity.
- Celebrate the Moments You Create, Not the Ones You Miss – Focus on your own experiences, not others' highlights.

- Realize That You're Not Actually Missing Anything – Trends fade, posts disappear, but your peace of mind stays.

  Key Takeaway: Missing out online means gaining more in real life.

Learning: Take Back Your Mental Space

You don't have to be "always online" to be informed, valued, or successful. True happiness isn't about knowing everything happening in the world—it's about being present in your own life.

Ask Yourself:

- What am I afraid of missing out on, and why?
- Does staying connected make me happy or anxious?
- How can I start embracing JOMO in my daily life?

Action Step: Try one full day without social media and see how you feel. You might just love the freedom!

CHAPTER 16

BREAKING FREE FROM DOPAMINE LOOPS

How to Reset Your Brain for Long-Term Digital Control

> *"The first step toward digital freedom is understanding that your brain is being hacked."*
>
> **– Nir Eyal**

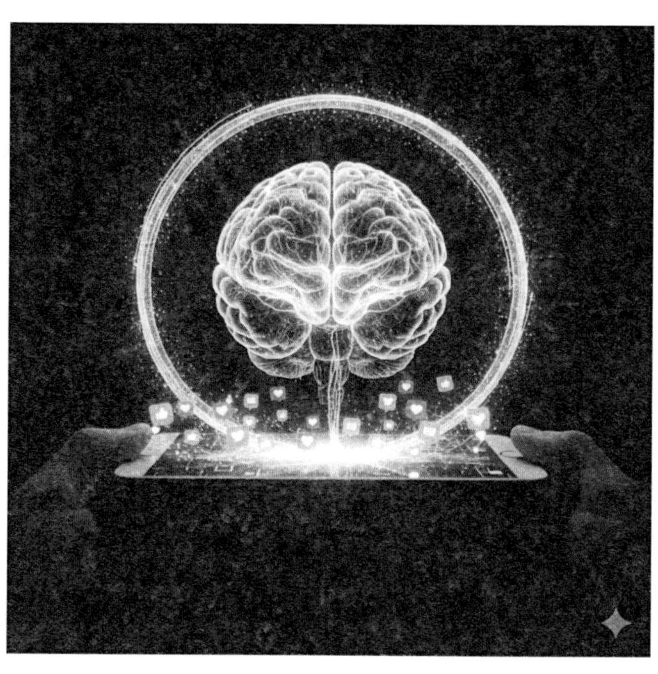

The apps you use every day—social media, video platforms, and even news sites—are not designed for your well-being. They are engineered to keep you hooked for as long as possible. The secret behind this addiction? Dopamine loops.

Dopamine is a neurotransmitter that creates feelings of pleasure and reward. Every time you receive a notification, like, or a new message, your brain releases a small hit of dopamine, reinforcing the urge to keep checking your device. Over time, this forms a habit loop, trapping you in a cycle of compulsive scrolling, checking, and refreshing.

The good news? You can rewire your brain and break free from this trap. In this chapter, we'll explore how dopamine loops control your behavior, how digital addiction rewires your brain, and the steps you can take to regain control over your technology use.

1. Understanding Dopamine Loops: The Science of Digital Addiction

What is Dopamine?

Dopamine is often called the "feel-good" chemical, but in reality, its job is not just to make you happy—it's to create cravings, anticipation, and motivation.

Healthy dopamine triggers: Exercise, learning, completing tasks, deep conversations.

Unhealthy dopamine triggers: Social media notifications, endless scrolling, autoplay videos, and viral content.

The Problem? Digital platforms exploit your dopamine system, making you crave more likes, messages, and new content—even when it doesn't make you happy.

2. How Digital Dopamine Loops Keep You Addicted

The Habit Loop: How It Works

- Trigger – You feel bored or anxious → You check your phone.
- Action – You scroll through social media or watch a short video.
- Reward – Your brain gets a dopamine hit from new content.
- Repeat – Your brain starts craving the next hit, making the habit stronger.

Examples of Dopamine Loops in Digital Addiction:

Social media: Refreshing for new likes, comments, or messages.

Video Platforms: Autoplay keeps you watching for hours.

News Feeds: Infinite scrolling keeps you hunting for something interesting.
Gaming & Gambling Apps: Reward systems (points, streaks, notifications) create addictive loops.

The more you indulge, the harder it is to stop. Your brain adapts by reducing its natural dopamine sensitivity, making you crave stronger digital stimulation over time.

3. How to Reset Your Brain & Break the Dopamine Addiction

Step 1: Identify Your Digital Dopamine Triggers

Ask Yourself:

When do I feel the strongest urge to check my phone?
Which apps or platforms do I use compulsively?
Do I feel satisfied after using them, or do I want more?
The Goal: Recognize your habits so you can disrupt them.

Step 2: Reduce Instant Gratification & Create Friction

- Turn Off Notifications – Reduce the urge to check for updates.
- Disable Autoplay – Stop binge-watching without thinking.
- Remove Addictive Apps from Your Home Screen – Make them harder to access.
- Set App Time Limits – Use tools like Freedom, Forest, or Screen Time to restrict usage.

The Goal: Make unhealthy dopamine triggers harder to access.

Step 3: Replace Digital Dopamine with Healthy Rewards

Instead of scrolling, try:
Exercise – Natural dopamine booster.
Deep Work & Learning – Engaging in challenging tasks increases real satisfaction.
Face-to-Face Socializing – Strengthens the brain's natural reward system.
Mindfulness & Meditation – Helps reset your focus and impulse control.

The Goal: Train your brain to crave real-life rewards instead of digital distractions.

Step 4: Try a Dopamine Detox to Reset Your Brain

What is a Dopamine Detox?

A dopamine detox is a temporary break from high-stimulation activities like social media, video games, and excessive screen time. This helps your brain reset its reward system and restore focus, patience, and self-control.

How to Do It:

Start with 24 hours without unnecessary digital stimulation.

Engage in low-dopamine activities like reading, journaling, walking, or deep conversations.
Slowly reintroduce technology with intention—use it as a tool, not a distraction.

The Goal: Reduce dependence on quick dopamine fixes and rebuild your ability to focus and enjoy deeper, long-term rewards.

Learning: Reclaiming Your Brain from Digital Control

Dopamine loops keep you trapped in digital addiction—but you have the power to break free. By understanding how technology hijacks your brain and making intentional changes, you can rewire your habits, regain focus, and take control of your digital life.

Ask Yourself:

- How is my screen time affecting my mental health and productivity?
- What changes can I make today to reduce digital overstimulation?
- What real-life activities can I prioritize over mindless scrolling?

Action Step: Try a 24-hour dopamine detox and see how your brain feels without digital distractions. Freedom starts with awareness!

DIGITAL MINIMALISM – LESS IS MORE

Using Technology with Intention, Not Addiction

> *"The key to a healthy relationship with technology isn't abstinence—it's intentionality."*
>
> **– Cal Newport**

We live in a world where more is always encouraged—more apps, more notifications, more content. But in reality, more digital consumption often leads to less mental clarity, less focus, and less real-life connection. The solution? Digital minimalism.

Digital minimalism is not about quitting technology; it's about using it with purpose. Instead of letting your devices control you, this philosophy helps you curate your digital life, removing distractions while keeping only what truly adds value.

In this chapter, we'll explore powerful tools, apps, and techniques that will help you reduce screen time, eliminate digital clutter, and create a tech-life balance that actually serves you.

1. Understanding Digital Minimalism: What It Means & Why It Matters

What is Digital Minimalism?

Using technology intentionally, not mindlessly.
Prioritizing quality over quantity in digital interactions.
Eliminating unnecessary apps, notifications, and distractions.
Creating boundaries for a healthier, more focused life.

Why is it Important?

- Regains Focus – Stops constant distraction and improves concentration.
- Reduces Anxiety – Less digital noise means better mental health.
- Saves Time – More time for meaningful offline activities.
- Improves Relationships – Reduces screen addiction and increases presence in real life.

Key Insight: Technology should serve you, not enslave you.

2. Step-by-Step Guide to Digital Minimalism

Step 1: Audit Your Digital Life

Before you declutter, analyze your current habits.

Ask Yourself:

Which apps do I spend the most time on? (Check Screen Time settings on your phone)
Do these apps add value or just waste time?
How often do I pick up my phone out of habit?
What are my biggest digital distractions?

Action Step: Write down your top 3 most time-consuming apps. Plan how to reduce or remove them.

Step 2: Declutter Your Digital Space

- Delete Unnecessary Apps – If you don't need it, remove it.
- Unfollow, Unsubscribe, uninstall – Unfollow accounts that don't add value, unsubscribe from useless emails, and uninstall apps that waste time.
- Clean Your Home Screen – Keep only essential apps visible. Move distractions to hidden folders.
- Organize Your Digital Files – Declutter old photos, documents, and emails.

The Goal: Make your digital environment simple and intentional.

Step 3: Set Boundaries with Technology

Use the 20-Second Rule – Make distractions harder to access (e.g., log out of social media).
Create "No-Screen Zones" – Avoid screens in the bedroom, at dinner, or during conversations.

Schedule Tech-Free Time – Set specific hours where you disconnect completely.
Turn Off Notifications – Reduce interruptions by keeping only essential alerts on.

Action Step: Set a daily screen limit for social media and stick to it.

3. Best Apps & Tools for Digital Minimalism

- App Blockers & Focus Tools (This is just a suggestion. No paid promotion)
  - Freedom – Blocks distracting apps/websites.
  - Forest – Encourages focus by growing virtual trees.
  - Stay Focused – Limits time on certain websites.
  - Cold Turkey – Completely locks access to distracting sites.
- Screen Time Trackers
  - Digital Wellbeing (Android) / Screen Time (iOS) – Tracks app usage and sets limits.
  - Rescue Time – Provides detailed reports on where your digital time goes.
  - One Sec – Forces a delay before opening addictive apps, breaking impulsive habits.
- Minimalist Reading & Learning Apps
  - Instapaper/Pocket – Saves articles for focused reading.
  - Kindle – Encourages reading instead of mindless scrolling.
  - Blinkist – Summarizes books to help you absorb key insights quickly.
- Email & Notification Management
  - Unroll.Me – Unsubscribes from junk emails easily.
  - Inbox When Ready – Hides your inbox to reduce distractions.
  - Boomerang – Schedules emails so you're not always online.

Note: These are just suggestions. The author is not promoting any app or website. Read reviews, terms, and conditions before moving ahead.

The Goal: Use apps that help you focus, not distract you.

4. Practicing Intentional Digital Consumption

How to Consume Digital Content Mindfully:
Follow Only High-Value Content Creators – Avoid mindless scrolling.
Replace Passive Scrolling with Active Learning – Read, listen to podcasts, or take online courses instead of watching random videos.
Apply the "1-Hour Rule" – Limit social media to a set time per day.
Use the "Digital Sabbath" – Take a full one-day break from screens every week.

The Goal: Be intentional about what you consume and how you engage online.

5. The Long-Term Benefits of Digital Minimalism

What Happens When You Use Technology with Purpose?
More Mental Clarity – Less clutter, more focus.
Better Productivity – No distractions = deeper work.
Stronger Relationships – More presence in conversations.
Improved Well-Being – Less stress, better sleep, more life satisfaction.

Key Insight: Minimalism isn't about removing technology—it's about using it wisely.

Learning: Take Control of Your Digital Life

Ask Yourself:

- What unnecessary digital habits can I cut today?
- How can I make my phone a tool for productivity, not a distraction?
- What boundaries can I set to reduce digital overwhelm?

Action Step: Try one week of digital minimalism—remove distractions, limit screen time, and observe how it changes your focus, mood, and life!

RECLAIMING FOCUS & MENTAL CLARITY

How to Restore Attention Span, Creativity, and Deep Thinking

> *"Your focus is your most valuable asset. Guard it fiercely."*
>
> **– Johann Hari**

In a world filled with endless notifications, social media feeds, and digital distractions, our ability to focus has become one of the biggest casualties of the digital age. We check our phones every few minutes, struggle to read long-form content, and find it hard to sit with our thoughts without reaching for a screen.

But here's the truth: Focus is a skill, not a fixed trait. The same way we lost it, we can rebuild it.

This chapter explores why our attention spans have declined, how digital distractions sabotage deep thinking, and most importantly, how to reclaim mental clarity for better productivity, creativity, and a richer life.

1. The Attention Crisis: How Digital Overload is Destroying Our Focus

What's Happening to Our Brains?

- The average person checks their phone over 150 times a day.
- The human attention span has dropped from 12 seconds in 2000 to around 8 seconds today—shorter than a goldfish.
- Digital multitasking reduces IQ by 10 points—as much as losing a full night's sleep.

Why?

Constant Dopamine Hits: Each notification or message gives a small dopamine reward, making us crave more interruptions.
Infinite Scrolling Culture: Apps like TikTok, Instagram, and Twitter are designed to keep us hooked.
Multitasking Overload: We switch between tasks too frequently, reducing deep thinking and creativity.

The Result? A scattered mind, poor concentration, and an inability to engage in deep, meaningful work.

2. How to Train Your Brain to Focus Again

Step 1: Strengthen Your Attention Muscle

- The 25-Minute Rule (Pomodoro Technique) – Work in focused 25-minute blocks, then take a 5-minute break. Repeat.
- Single-Tasking Over Multitasking – Focus on one task at a time. Switching between tasks reduces efficiency by 40%.
- Use the "Do Not Disturb" Mode – Silence non-essential notifications to avoid distractions.
- Train with Deep Work Sessions – Set a timer and work without interruptions (start with 30 minutes, increase gradually).

The Goal: Improve sustained focus and train your brain for longer periods of concentration.

Step 2: Declutter Your Digital Environment

Turn Off Push Notifications – No more dopamine traps.
Limit Social Media Usage – Set specific time slots for checking apps instead of mindless browsing.
Use Website Blockers – Apps like Freedom, Cold Turkey, or StayFocusd can block distracting sites.
Create a Minimalist Desktop & Phone Layout – Keep only essential apps on the home screen.

The Goal: Reduce temptation and free up mental space for creativity and deep thought.

Step 3: Strengthen Your Mind Through Deep Thinking Practices

How to Improve Cognitive Clarity:

- Read Long-Form Content – Instead of short tweets, commit to books, essays, and deep articles.
- Write by Hand – Journaling or brainstorming on paper improves retention and critical thinking.
- Engage in Slow Conversations – Deep, meaningful conversations train your brain for patience and focus.
- Practice Reflection & Solitude – Spend time alone without a screen to regain mental clarity.

The Goal: Rewire your brain for deep thought and complex problem-solving.

3. The Link Between Creativity & Focus

Why Digital Distraction Kills Creativity:

Creativity requires boredom – Constant entertainment eliminates mental space for new ideas.
Excessive screen time reduces divergent thinking – The ability to explore multiple ideas at once.
Overuse of social media creates comparison anxiety – Blocking true self-expression.

How to Restore Creativity:

Schedule Screen-Free Brainstorming Time – Disconnect and let your mind wander.
Engage in Creative Hobbies – Painting, writing, or music helps train the mind to focus deeply.
Take Breaks in Nature – Studies show spending time outdoors improves creative problem-solving by 50%.
The Goal: Make space for deep creativity instead of constant consumption.

4. The Power of Mindfulness & Meditation in Regaining Focus

How Mindfulness Helps:

Improves attention control – Training the mind to focus on the present.
Reduces stress & mental clutter – Making thinking clearer.
Strengthens impulse control – Less automatic checking of notifications.

Simple Techniques to Try:

- 5-Minute Breathing Exercise – Sit quietly, focus on your breath, and observe your thoughts.
- Single-Tasking Mindfully – When eating, walking, or listening, be fully present.
- Guided Meditation Apps – Use tools like Headspace or Calm for structured mindfulness practice.

The Goal: Train your mind to be fully engaged in the present moment.

5. Designing a Focus-Friendly Daily Routine

Morning (Digital-Free Start) – Avoid checking your phone for the first 30 minutes.
Deep Work Block (2-4 hours of Uninterrupted Focus) – No distractions, no notifications.
Mindful Breaks (Every 90 Minutes) – Step away from screens and reset.
Evening Digital Detox – No screens at least 1 hour before bed to improve sleep.

The Goal: Build daily habits that protect and enhance your focus.

Learning: Take Back Control of Your Attention

Ask Yourself:

- How often do I get distracted while working or reading?
- What small changes can I make today to improve my attention span?
- How can I design my environment to support focus and deep thinking?

Action Step: Try one full day without social media and notifications—see how your mind feels without digital noise.

Remember: Your attention is your most valuable asset. Use it wisely!

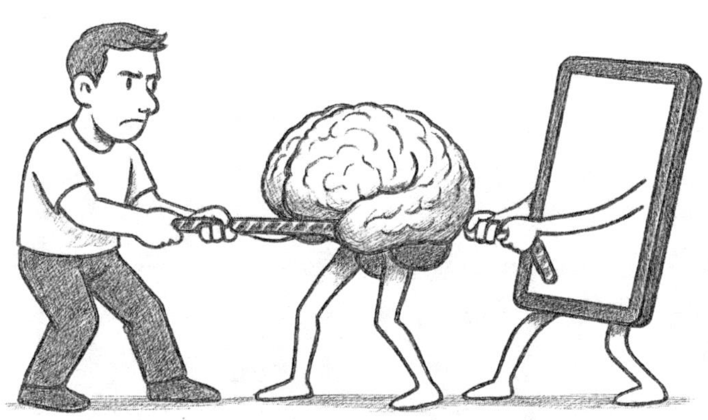

THE ART OF MINDFUL TECHNOLOGY USE

Learning to Use Tech Without Being Controlled by It

> *"Do not dwell in the past, do not dream of the future, concentrate the mind on the present moment."*
>
> **– Buddha**

In today's hyperconnected world, technology is embedded in nearly every aspect of our lives. From work emails to social media updates, from binge-watching shows to endless scrolling, we are constantly engaged with our devices. But the real question is: Are we using technology, or is technology using us?

Mindful technology use is about being intentional and conscious about our screen habits. Instead of mindless scrolling, compulsive checking, and digital distractions, it's about making choices that serve our well-being, productivity, and real-life relationships.

This chapter will explore how to develop a healthier, more balanced relationship with technology—one where you stay in control, rather than being controlled.

1. What is Mindful Technology Use?

Mindfulness means awareness and intention.

Mindful technology use is about:

Using devices with purpose instead of habit.
Recognizing when technology adds value vs. when it's a distraction.
Setting boundaries to prevent digital overwhelm.
Creating a tech-life balance that enhances well-being.

Why is this important?

- More focus – Less distraction means deeper work.
- Better mental health – Less comparison, anxiety, and stress.
- Improved relationships – More real-life presence, fewer digital intrusions.
- Increased productivity – Using tech efficiently rather than being consumed by it.

Key Insight: Technology should be a tool that enhances life—not an addiction that steals it.

2. The Difference Between Intentional & Compulsive Tech Use

Intentional Use:

Checking messages with a purpose, then logging off.
Using social media to connect, not just for endless scrolling.
Scheduling screen time instead of letting it take over.
Using apps that improve productivity and well-being.

Compulsive Use:

Checking notifications first thing in the morning out of habit.
Mindlessly scrolling through feeds for hours without realizing it.
Feeling anxious when away from the phone.
Letting screens replace real-life social interactions.

The Goal: Shift from compulsive to conscious tech habits.

3. How to Cultivate Mindful Technology Habits

Step 1: Create Intentional Tech Routines

- Set "Check-In" Times – Instead of constantly checking emails or social media, schedule specific times for them (e.g., twice a day).
- Use "Focus Mode" on Devices – Many smartphones have digital well-being settings to block distractions.
- Tech-Free Mornings & Evenings – Avoid screens 30 minutes after waking up and 1 hour before bed.
- Mindful Social Media Use – Before opening an app, ask: "Why am I here?" If there's no clear reason, don't scroll.

Action Step: Try a "No Notifications Day" once a week—see how it changes your focus and mindset.

Step 2: Design a Distraction-Free Environment

Turn Off Non-Essential Notifications – Only keep alerts for important messages.
Use a Minimalist Home Screen – Keep only the apps you need; move distractions to hidden folders.
Charge Your Phone Outside the Bedroom – Avoid late-night scrolling and improve sleep.
Set Time Limits for Apps – Use tools like Digital Wellbeing (Android), Screen Time (iOS), or Freedom.

The Goal: Make distractions harder to access and focus easier to maintain.

Step 3: Practice Digital Mindfulness

How to Be More Present in Tech Use:

- Before Using Your Phone, Pause & Breathe – Ask: Do I really need to check this?
- Consume Content Consciously – Avoid mindless scrolling; choose meaningful content.
- Take Digital Detox Breaks – Even short breaks improve mental clarity.
- Set "Phone-Free" Zones – Keep devices away during meals, social gatherings, and deep work sessions.

Action Step: Try the "One-Screen Rule" – Use only one screen at a time (e.g., no TV + phone scrolling).

4. Mindful Technology Use for Work & Productivity

How to Use Tech for Efficiency, Not Overload:
Batch Process Emails – Instead of constantly checking, respond in set time slots.
Use the "Two-Minute Rule" – If a task takes less than 2 minutes, do it immediately instead of letting digital clutter build up.
Turn Off Work Notifications After Hours – Separate work and personal life.
Use Productivity Apps – Tools like Notion, Trello, or Evernote help streamline digital workflows.

The Goal: Use technology to enhance productivity, not overwhelm you.

5. The Role of Mindful Tech Use in Relationships

The Problem: Many people spend more time on screens than engaging with loved ones.

How to Be More Present in Relationships:
No-Phone Rule at Meals – Keep conversations screen-free.
Set "Tech-Free" Date Nights – Spend quality time without digital distractions.
Be Fully Present – When talking to someone, put the phone away and give them your full attention.
Encourage Offline Activities – Engage in hobbies, sports, and social interactions that don't involve screens.

The Goal: Strengthen real-life connections by reducing digital intrusions.

6. Tools & Apps for Mindful Technology Use

- Digital Detox & Focus Apps
  - Forest – Helps you stay off your phone by growing virtual trees.
  - Freedom – Blocks distracting apps and websites.
  - StayFocusd – Limits time on addictive sites.
- Screen Time Management
  - Digital Wellbeing (Android) / Screen Time (iOS) – Tracks phone usage and sets app limits.
  - Rescue Time – Provides insights on where your digital time goes.
- Conscious Content Consumption
  - Pocket/Instapaper – Saves articles for later, reducing impulsive browsing.
  - Kindle & Audiobooks – Encourages deep reading instead of short-form scrolling.

The Goal: Use apps that help you control your tech habits, not ones that control you.

Learning: Becoming the Master of Your Tech Use

Ask Yourself:

- Do I control my technology, or does it control me?
- How often do I use my phone out of habit rather than necessity?
- What changes can I make to use technology more mindfully?

Action Step: Try a 24-hour mindful tech challenge—only use devices with intention, no mindless scrolling or notifications. See how it feels!

Remember: Technology should be your tool, not your distraction. Use it wisely!

HOW TO HANDLE PEER PRESSURE & SOCIAL EXPECTATIONS

Resisting Digital Addiction in a Hyper-Connected World

> *"The greatest prison people live in is the fear of what other people think."*
>
> – **David Icke**

In today's world, staying constantly connected is often seen as a social norm. If you don't reply instantly to messages, people assume you're ignoring them. If you're not active on social media, you might feel like you're missing out or being left behind. The pressure to stay online, stay visible, and stay engaged can feel overwhelming.

Peer pressure and social expectations play a major role in why so many people struggle to break free from digital addiction. Whether it's the pressure to be available 24/7, to participate in online trends, or to present a perfect digital persona, the fear of missing out (FOMO) and social validation can keep us glued to our screens—even when we know it's unhealthy.

But the good news is: You can resist digital peer pressure and take control of your online habits. This chapter will explore how to navigate social expectations, set boundaries, and stay true to yourself in a world that constantly demands your digital attention.

1. Understanding Digital Peer Pressure

Peer pressure doesn't just happen in real-life interactions; it's equally powerful in the digital world.

Common Forms of Digital Peer Pressure:

- **Always Being Available** – Feeling obligated to reply immediately to messages, emails, or group chats.
- **Social Media Validation** – The pressure to post regularly and get likes, comments, and shares.
- **Following Trends** – Feeling forced to engage in viral challenges, online debates, or new apps.
- **FOMO (Fear of Missing Out)** – The anxiety of not keeping up with online discussions, events, or updates.

- **Comparing Your Life to Others** – The feeling that everyone else has a more exciting, successful, or glamorous life.

The Impact:
Increases screen time and compulsive social media use.
Creates anxiety, stress, and low self-esteem.
Distracts from real-life relationships and experiences.

The Truth: Just because "everyone is doing it" doesn't mean it's right, necessary, or healthy for you.

2. How to Recognize & Resist Digital Peer Pressure

Step 1: Identify Your Triggers

- Ask yourself:

Do I check my phone because I want to—or because I feel pressured?
Am I posting something just to get validation?
Do I feel anxious if I don't check social media for a few hours?

Action Step: Keep a digital journal for a few days. Write down when and why you check your phone or social media. Recognizing your patterns is the first step to breaking free.

Step 2: Set Healthy Digital Boundaries

You don't have to be available 24/7 just because society expects it. Your time and attention are yours to control.

Response Time Boundaries – Let people know you don't reply instantly to messages.
Social Media Detox Days – Take scheduled breaks from social platforms.
No-Phone Zones – Create tech-free areas (e.g., during meals, before bed).
Unfollow Toxic Accounts – If a page or person makes you feel pressured or inadequate, unfollow them.

Action Step: Start small—try turning off notifications for a day and see how it changes your behavior.

Step 3: Build Real-Life Connections & Confidence

The best way to resist digital peer pressure is to create a fulfilling life outside of screens.

Strengthen Offline Friendships – Meet people in person instead of only through chat.
Engage in Hobbies – Sports, reading, art, music—things that bring you joy without a screen.
Develop Self-Confidence – When you feel secure in yourself, you don't need digital validation.

Action Step: Plan a real-life activity with friends or family this week that doesn't involve screens.

3. Overcoming FOMO & Digital Anxiety

FOMO (Fear of Missing Out) is an illusion. Social media only shows the highlights of people's lives, not the full picture.

How to Overcome FOMO:

Practice Gratitude – Focus on what's happening in your own life, not what others are doing.
Limit Social Media Time – The less time you spend online, the less you compare.
Be Present in the Moment – Enjoy where you are instead of wishing you were somewhere else.
Replace FOMO with JOMO (Joy of Missing Out) – Find happiness in disconnecting and focusing on yourself.

The Truth: You're not missing out—you're gaining time, focus, and mental clarity.

4. Dealing with Social Pressure to Stay Online

What if people expect you to always be available?

Be Honest About Your Digital Boundaries

- Let people know you're reducing screen time for your well-being.
- Explain that you're not ignoring them—you're just prioritizing your mental health.

Don't Feel Guilty for Logging Off

- You are not obligated to respond to every message or comment instantly.
- True friends will respect your choices, not pressure you.

Set Auto-Replies for Messages

- Use "Do Not Disturb" or auto-reply settings to let people know when you're unavailable.

Action Step: Try a "Silent Sunday"—one full day without social media. Let people know in advance. See how you feel!

5. Redefining Success & Happiness in a Digital Age

True success isn't about followers, likes, or online presence. It's about real-life happiness, meaningful connections, and personal growth.

How to Define Your Own Success:
Focus on personal goals, not social media validation.
Measure your success by growth, learning, and relationships—not digital attention.
Prioritize real-life experiences over virtual ones.

The Goal: Live for yourself, not for social media.

Learning: Take Control of Your Digital Life

Ask Yourself:

- Am I using technology for my benefit, or am I following social pressure?
- Do I make decisions based on what others expect or what truly makes me happy?
- What steps can I take today to reduce digital peer pressure in my life?

Action Step: Challenge yourself to a 7-day mindful tech use experiment. Reduce unnecessary screen time, avoid social validation traps, and focus on real-life moments.

Remember: Your life is yours. Don't let digital expectations define it!

PART 3

EMBRACING A NEW LIFESTYLE

21. The Joy of Real-Life Connections – Strengthening relationships outside the screen.
22. Hobbies, Passions & Real-World Activities – Discovering fulfilling alternatives to digital distractions.
23. Raising Tech-Smart Kids – Parenting strategies to protect children from screen addiction.
24. The Role of Schools & Educators in Digital Wellness – How education can help in creating responsible digital citizens.
25. The Digital Sabbath: Unplugging Regularly – Practicing screen-free days for a balanced life.
26. How Companies Can Support Digital Wellness – Workplace strategies for reducing digital fatigue.
27. Reconnecting with Nature & the Outdoors – The healing power of nature in breaking digital dependency.
28. Building a Long-Term Digital Detox Plan – Sustainable strategies for a tech-healthy future.
29. A Life of Presence & Purpose – The ultimate reward of a digital detox lifestyle.
30. The Future of Technology & Human Well-Being – How to create a balanced digital future without addiction.

THE JOY OF REAL-LIFE CONNECTIONS

Strengthening Relationships Outside the Screen

> *"Connection is why we're here; it is what gives purpose and meaning to our lives."*
>
> **– Brené Brown**

In an era where conversations are replaced by texts, laughter is expressed through emojis, and relationships exist within pixels, we have slowly drifted away from what truly makes us human—genuine, real-life connections.

The irony of the digital age is that while we are more connected than ever before, we've never felt more disconnected. Families sit together but stare at their screens. Friends meet but barely talk. Parents and children live under the same roof, yet exist in different virtual worlds. We are losing the art of presence, the depth of relationships, and the warmth of face-to-face interactions.

But what if we could reclaim the joy of real-life connections? This chapter will explore why human relationships thrive beyond screens and how we can restore the depth, intimacy, and meaning in our social interactions.

1. The Digital Disconnection Crisis

Technology was meant to bring us closer, but it has created invisible walls.

How Screens Have Distanced Us:

- Phantom Presence: We may be physically present, but our minds are elsewhere—lost in notifications and scrolling.
- Superficial Conversations: Digital interactions lack the depth and emotional richness of face-to-face discussions.
- Less Empathy & Understanding: Without tone, facial expressions, and body language, online communication often leads to misunderstandings.
- Quality Time Replaced by Screen Time: Meaningful family dinners, heart-to-heart talks, and spontaneous moments are disappearing.

Reflection: When was the last time you had a distraction-free conversation with a loved one?

2. Why Real-Life Connections Matter

The human brain is wired for deep social bonds. No amount of texting or video calls can replace the emotional satisfaction of in-person interactions.

Face-to-Face Interactions Strengthen Relationships

- 90% of communication is non-verbal (body language, tone, facial expressions).
- Real-life conversations build stronger trust and deeper understanding.

Spending Time with Loved Ones Improves Mental Health

- Studies show that social interactions reduce stress, anxiety, and depression.
- Laughing, hugging, and talking in person release oxytocin—the "bonding hormone."

Physical Presence Creates Lasting Memories

- Moments spent together in real life stay in our hearts forever. A like or a comment on a post? Easily forgotten.

Action Step: Make eye contact, smile, and engage deeply in your next conversation—without a phone in sight.

3. How to Rebuild Real-Life Relationships in a Digital World

Step 1: Be Fully Present

The best gift you can give someone is your undivided attention.

Put your phone away during conversations.
Listen actively—without checking messages or scrolling.

Make time for in-person meetups instead of just chatting online.

Challenge: Try the "Phone-Free Hour" every day—dedicate one hour to uninterrupted connection with a loved one.

Step 2: Prioritize Real-Life Over Virtual Life

Your relationships should exist beyond screens.

Choose calls over texts, and meet-ups over DMs.
Plan outings, activities, or casual hangouts instead of endless online chats.
Spend weekends engaging in outdoor activities instead of binge-scrolling.

Action Step: Call or visit a friend instead of texting them today.

Step 3: Create Tech-Free Zones & Rituals

Small habits can transform relationships.

Family Meals Without Screens – Make dinner time a sacred bonding moment.
Screen-Free Bedtime Routine – Talk, read, or unwind with loved ones without distractions.
Weekend Digital Detox – Dedicate time for outdoor activities, hobbies, and real interactions.

Action Step: Start with a "Tech-Free Dinner Challenge" tonight!

4. Finding Joy in Offline Moments

What if the best moments in life aren't captured on a screen but felt in the heart?

Go on unplanned adventures.
Laugh without worrying about capturing it for social media.
Have deep conversations that don't need to be shared online.
Be present in life's little joys—sunsets, hugs, shared meals, and laughter.

The Truth: Life's most precious moments don't need a digital audience.

Action Step: Enjoy one special moment today—fully present, without a screen.

Learning: Choose Real Life Over Virtual Life

In a world constantly pulling us towards screens, choose to be different. Choose to live, feel, and connect beyond the digital world.

Ask Yourself:

- Am I more invested in my online presence than my real-life relationships?
- When was the last time I truly connected with someone, uninterrupted?
- What steps can I take today to strengthen my offline relationships?

Challenge: Try a "Weekend Without Social Media" and rediscover the beauty of real-life connections!

Remember: The best moments in life happen when you're truly present. Make them count.

HOBBIES, PASSIONS & REAL-WORLD ACTIVITIES

Discovering Fulfilling Alternatives to Digital Distractions

> *"The secret of happiness is not in doing what one likes, but in liking what one does."*
>
> **– James M. Barrie**

In today's hyper-connected world, many people fill every free moment with screen time—scrolling through social media, binge-watching videos, or endlessly checking notifications. But have you ever stopped to ask: What would I do if I didn't have a phone in my hand?

The truth is, digital distractions have robbed us of real-world passions. Many of us used to enjoy hobbies like painting, reading, playing music, or outdoor sports, but now those activities have been replaced by passive scrolling and screen addiction.

But here's the good news: You can reclaim your time, rediscover old passions, and explore new, meaningful activities that bring real joy and fulfillment. This chapter will help you break free from digital dependency and replace screen time with hobbies and real-world experiences that enrich your life.

1. The Cost of Digital Distractions

Why do we default to screens instead of real-world activities?

- Instant Gratification: social media and digital content provide quick, effortless entertainment.
- Mindless Escapism: People turn to screens to avoid boredom, stress, or real-life challenges.
- Fear of Missing Out (FOMO): The belief that staying offline means missing something important.
- Lack of Time & Energy: Work and responsibilities drain people, making screen-based entertainment feel "easier" than active hobbies.

The Result?
Wasted time with nothing meaningful to show for it.
Reduced creativity, productivity, and self-improvement.
Weaker real-world social skills and fewer personal achievements.

The Truth: Your free time is precious—don't let it be consumed by mindless digital habits!

2. Rediscovering the Joy of Offline Activities

Ask yourself:

What did I love doing as a child or teenager before screens took over?
What real-world activities make me feel engaged, happy, or accomplished?
If I had to spend a weekend without screens, what would I do instead?

Action Step: Write down three non-digital activities you enjoy or would like to try.

3. Hobbies & Activities That Replace Digital Dependency

Here are some fulfilling alternatives to screen time:

- Creative Hobbies (Boost Your Imagination & Self-Expression)

    Painting, drawing, or sculpting
    Creative writing or journaling
    Playing a musical instrument
    Photography (without excessive social media posting!)

- Physical & Outdoor Activities (Boost Energy & Mental Clarity)

    Hiking, jogging, or cycling
    Yoga, meditation, or dance
    Team sports or martial arts
    Gardening or outdoor adventures

- Intellectual Growth Activities (Expand Your Knowledge & Skills)

Reading books (fiction, non-fiction, self-improvement)
Learning a new language
Solving puzzles, chess, or brain games
Taking online courses (but limiting unnecessary screen use)

- Social & Community Engagement (Strengthen Real-Life Connections)

  Volunteering for a cause you care about
  Joining a book club or creative group
  Organizing game nights or social meetups
  Spending more time with family and friends (without screens!)

4. Replacing Digital Dopamine with Real-World Fulfillment

Why are hobbies more rewarding than digital distractions?

They give a sense of achievement. Unlike passive scrolling, real hobbies allow you to create, improve, and grow.

They reduce stress and improve focus. Engaging in non-digital activities enhances mental clarity and emotional well-being.

They provide real-world social interactions. Hobbies help you connect with like-minded people in meaningful ways.

They increase self-confidence. Mastering a new skill or hobby gives a deep sense of personal fulfillment.

Action Step: Challenge yourself to spend at least one hour per day on a real-world hobby instead of digital distractions.

5. How to Make Time for Hobbies in a Digital World

Overcoming common excuses:

"I don't have time." → Reduce unnecessary screen time and schedule hobbies like appointments.

"I don't know what I like." → Experiment with different activities until you find one that excites you.

"I'm not good at anything." → Every expert started as a beginner—just start!

Practical Tips:

Schedule Hobby Time – Treat hobbies as essential, not optional.

Reduce Digital Noise – Limit social media and screen time to free up hours for real activities.

Find a Hobby Buddy – Engaging in activities with friends makes them more enjoyable and consistent.

Learning: Make Life More Than Just Screens

Your time is valuable. Spend it on activities that enrich your mind, body, and soul.

Challenge: For the next 7 days, swap at least one hour of screen time for a real-world hobby. Notice how it changes your mood, focus, and happiness!

Remember: True joy comes from doing, creating, and experiencing life—not just consuming digital content.

CHAPTER 23

RAISING TECH-SMART KIDS

Parenting Strategies to Protect Children from Screen Addiction

> *"Don't let your kids play with smartphones. We don't know the consequences."*
>
> – **Steve Jobs**

In today's digital age, screens are everywhere, and children are introduced to technology before they can even walk or talk. Tablets, smartphones, YouTube, and gaming apps have become digital babysitters, offering instant entertainment at the tap of a screen. However, this convenience comes at a cost—rising screen addiction, declining attention spans, and emotional disconnect from the real world.

As a parent, you want to give your child the best of both worlds: the benefits of technology without its harmful effects. But how do you achieve this balance when screens are such an integral part of modern life?

This chapter will provide practical, research-backed strategies to help parents raise tech-smart kids—children who use technology wisely without becoming slaves to screens.

1. The Reality of Childhood Screen Addiction

Why are kids so drawn to screens?

- Instant gratification: Digital content is designed to keep kids hooked with endless autoplay and interactive features.
- Parental reliance: Busy parents often use screens to keep children occupied.
- Peer pressure: Kids feel the need to use devices because "everyone else is."
- Lack of outdoor & creative activities: With fewer real-world experiences, children naturally turn to digital entertainment.

The Impact:

Shorter attention spans and difficulty focusing in school.
Increased anxiety, mood swings, and behavioral issues.
Reduced physical activity that leads to obesity and poor health.
Weakened social skills and emotional intelligence.

The Truth: Technology is not the enemy—uncontrolled and excessive use is.

2. Understanding a Child's Relationship with Technology

Not all screen time is equal. A child watching an educational documentary for 30 minutes is different from mindlessly scrolling TikTok for hours.

Positive Screen Time:

- Learning apps and educational content
- Creative activities like coding, music production, or storytelling
- Family-friendly movies or games played together

Negative Screen Time:

- Endless social media scrolling
- Addictive video games with no limits
- Passive binge-watching with no mental engagement

Action Step: Start tracking how your child uses screens—what they watch, for how long, and its impact on their mood.

3. How to Set Healthy Digital Boundaries

Creating rules and limits is the first step to raising tech-smart kids.

1. Set Screen Time Limits
    - Follow the "No More Than 1 Hour of Recreational Screen Time" rule for young children.
    - For older kids, ensure screens do not interfere with sleep, school, or outdoor activities.

2. Establish Screen-Free Zones
   - No screens during family meals, bedtime, and social gatherings.
   - Keep devices out of bedrooms to ensure better sleep.
3. Model Healthy Tech Use as a Parent
   - Kids imitate parents. If you're always on your phone, they will be too.
   - Be mindful of your own screen habits.
4. Replace Screens with Engaging Activities
   - Encourage hobbies like reading, sports, music, and creative play.
   - Organize outdoor family outings to make real-world experiences exciting.

Challenge: Introduce a "Tech-Free Family Night" once a week—play games, cook together, or go for a walk instead of using screens.

4. Teaching Digital Responsibility & Awareness

Kids should learn that technology is a tool, not a necessity.

1. Teach the Importance of Delayed Gratification
   - Explain how apps and games are designed to be addictive.
   - Help them understand the benefits of patience and real-world engagement.
2. Have Open Conversations About Online Dangers
   - Discuss cyberbullying, online predators, and privacy concerns.
   - Teach kids to question content and recognize misinformation.
3. Encourage Active Screen Use
   - Instead of passive scrolling, guide them towards creating, learning, and exploring with technology.
   - Help them explore productive activities like coding, designing, and storytelling.

Action Step: Sit down with your child and talk about their screen habits. Ask them how they feel after long screen sessions versus outdoor play.

5. Raising Children Who Are in Control of Technology (Not the Other Way Around!)

The goal is to raise children who see technology as a helpful tool—not a source of addiction.

- Teach balance: Let kids enjoy tech, but also prioritize outdoor play, reading, and face-to-face interactions.
- Encourage critical thinking: Help them analyze and question what they see online.
- Foster self-control: Teach kids to take breaks and practice mindful screen usage.

Final Challenge: Ask your child to go one entire day without screens. Observe how they react and use it as a teaching moment about digital balance.

Learning: Raising a Tech-Smart Generation

Parenting in the digital age is challenging, but you have the power to shape your child's relationship with technology. Instead of fighting screens, teach kids how to use them wisely.

Key Takeaways:

Set clear boundaries and screen-free zones.
Encourage real-world hobbies and outdoor play.
Teach kids about digital responsibility and online dangers.
Be a role model—your habits influence theirs.

Remember: Your child's future depends on how they learn to interact with technology today. Let's raise a generation that controls screens—not the other way around.

THE ROLE OF SCHOOLS & EDUCATORS IN DIGITAL WELLNESS

How Education Can Help in Creating Responsible Digital Citizens

> *"Technology can become the 'wings' that will allow the educational world to fly farther and faster than ever before—if we allow it."*
>
> **– Jenny Arledge**

Technology has revolutionized education, making learning more accessible, interactive, and engaging. However, it has also introduced new challenges—students distracted by screens, cyberbullying, misinformation, and a growing dependency on digital devices.

While parents play a crucial role in shaping children's digital habits, schools and educators are equally responsible for teaching digital wellness. Just as schools educate students on subjects like math and science, they must also equip them with the skills to navigate the digital world responsibly.

This chapter explores how schools can create a balanced, mindful approach to technology while preparing students to be responsible digital citizens.

1. The Need for Digital Wellness in Schools

Why should schools actively teach digital wellness?

- Excessive screen time is affecting academic performance. Many students struggle with focus and retention due to constant digital distractions.
- Cyberbullying and online harassment are increasing. Children and teens face emotional distress from toxic online environments.
- Students lack media literacy skills. Many cannot distinguish between real and fake news, making them vulnerable to misinformation.
- Mental health concerns are rising. Social media pressure contributes to anxiety, depression, and low self-esteem.

The Role of Schools: Help students use technology effectively while avoiding its harmful effects.

2. Integrating Digital Wellness into Education

Schools must go beyond just teaching students how to use technology—they must teach them how to use it responsibly.

1. Digital Literacy Education
   - Teach students how the internet works, how algorithms shape content, and how to verify information.
   - Introduce critical thinking skills to help students question online content and avoid misinformation.
2. Mindful Screen Time Management
   - Implement guidelines for healthy tech usage in classrooms to prevent distractions.
   - Encourage students to take regular "tech breaks" to reset their focus.
3. Cyber Safety & Digital Citizenship Programs
   - Educate students on online privacy, cyberbullying, and responsible social media behavior.
   - Teach them about strong passwords, phishing attacks, and data protection.

Action Step: Schools should introduce mandatory digital wellness lessons alongside traditional subjects.

3. The Role of Teachers in Promoting Digital Balance

Teachers play a key role in shaping students' digital habits.

1. Setting a Positive Example
   - Teachers should model healthy tech use by minimizing screen distractions in classrooms.
   - Encourage students to engage in face-to-face discussions instead of relying on digital communication.

2. Encouraging Offline Activities
   - Promote reading physical books, creative projects, and outdoor activities over excessive screen-based assignments.
   - Introduce tech-free classroom discussions to enhance critical thinking and interpersonal skills.

3. Teaching the Consequences of Digital Addiction
   - Discuss the effects of dopamine-driven screen habits and their impact on mental health.
   - Help students understand how social media affects self-esteem and emotional well-being.

Challenge: Schools should implement "No-Phone Zones" in classrooms to encourage focused learning.

4. Implementing School-Wide Digital Wellness Policies

What can schools do to ensure a balanced approach to technology?

1. Establish Clear Screen Time Policies
   - Limit the use of non-educational screen time during school hours.
   - Encourage handwritten assignments and book-based learning to reduce digital dependency.

2. Host Digital Detox & Awareness Campaigns
   - Organize "Screen-Free Days" where students engage in offline learning activities.
   - Conduct workshops on social media addiction, gaming disorders, and mindfulness.

3. Partner with Parents
   - Schools should work with parents to create consistent digital wellness habits at home.

- Provide resources to help families set digital boundaries and manage screen time.

Action Step: Schools can introduce a "Mindful Technology Pledge" where students commit to using tech responsibly.

5. Preparing Students for a Digital Future

Technology is here to stay—our goal should be to help students use it wisely.

- Instead of banning screens, teach students how to use them mindfully.
- Encourage curiosity, creativity, and critical thinking in digital spaces.
- Equip students with the skills to balance technology with real-world interactions.

Final Challenge: Schools should encourage students to complete a "Digital Wellness Project"—where they track and analyze their screen time, identify distractions, and create personalized digital detox plans.

Learning: Schools as the Foundation for Digital Well-Being

Education is not just about teaching facts—it's about preparing students for life. In today's digital age, this means helping them develop a healthy relationship with technology.

Key Takeaways:
Schools should integrate digital wellness education into their curriculum.
Teachers must set an example of mindful tech use.
Schools need clear policies on screen time and digital citizenship.
Parents and educators must work together to guide children toward balanced tech habits.

Remember: A tech-smart generation starts with a tech-smart education. By teaching digital wellness, schools can shape responsible, mindful digital citizens who control technology—rather than being controlled by it.

THE DIGITAL FAST – UNPLUGGING REGULARLY

Practicing Screen-Free Days for a Balanced Life

> *"Almost everything will work again if you unplug it for a few minutes, including you."*
>
> – **Anne Lamott**

The Concept of Fasting: A Sacred Pause for Renewal

For centuries, fasting has been practiced across religions and cultures as a way to develop self-discipline, cleanse the body, and achieve mental and spiritual clarity. While fasting is commonly associated with food, the deeper meaning is about temporary abstinence from something habitual to regain control over it.

In the digital age, technology has become an addiction, making it essential to apply the principles of fasting to our screen habits. A Digital Fast is the modern equivalent of this ancient practice—a break from screens to restore focus, presence, and well-being.

Fasting Traditions Across Cultures

Hindu Upvas (Vrat) – Discipline & Purification
In Hinduism, fasting (Upvas or Vrat) is a way to cleanse both body and mind, practiced on Ekadashi, Navratri, Shivratri, or other auspicious days. It helps develop self-control, patience, and mindfulness—qualities that can also help in overcoming digital addiction.

The Christian Sabbath – A Day of Rest
The Sabbath, observed on Sundays in Christianity, is meant to be a day of worship, reflection, and detachment from worldly distractions. Many religious followers abstain from unnecessary work and focus on faith, family, and inner peace. A digital fast aligns with this principle, offering a modern-day Sabbath from screens.

Islamic Fasting (Ramadan) – Resisting Temptation
During Ramadan, Muslims fast from sunrise to sunset, developing self-restraint and awareness of their habits. The lesson is clear: we can train our minds to resist urges—including the compulsive need to check our phones.

These traditions teach us that temporary abstinence from something habitual leads to greater self-awareness and control. In the same way, a break from digital distractions can help reset our relationship with technology.

1. What is a Digital Fast?

A Digital Fast is a conscious break from digital devices—smartphones, social media, emails, and screens—to restore mental clarity, reduce stress, and reclaim focus.

- It's not about rejecting technology but about using it intentionally.
- It can last a few hours, a full day, or even an entire weekend.
- The goal is simple: Break free from digital dependency and reconnect with real life.

Challenge: *Can you go 12 hours without checking your phone?*

2. Why Do You Need a Digital Fast?

We are drowning in digital noise. A Digital Fast helps restore balance.

1. Reduces Stress & Anxiety
    - Notifications, emails, and social media overload our brains.
    - Taking a break allows us to breathe, relax, and find peace.
2. Improves Focus & Productivity
    - Constant digital distractions shorten attention spans.
    - Unplugging helps in deep work, problem-solving, and creativity.
3. Strengthens Relationships
    - Technology has replaced human connection.
    - A Digital Fast brings back meaningful face-to-face interactions.

4. Enhances Creativity & Self-Reflection
   - Without screens, the mind has space for new ideas and deep thinking.
   - Many successful people take digital breaks for clarity and inspiration.
5. Improves Sleep & Health
   - Screens, especially before bed, disrupt sleep cycles.
   - Less screen time means better sleep, posture, and overall well-being.

Ask Yourself: *Am I in control of my phone, or is my phone controlling me?*

3. How to Practice a Digital Fast

You don't need to quit technology forever—just take intentional breaks.

Step 1: Choose Your Digital Fast Duration

- Start with 4-6 hours of no screen time.
- Progress to a full day or even an entire weekend once a month.

Step 2: Set Clear Boundaries

- Inform family, friends, and colleagues in advance.
- Use "Do Not Disturb" mode or set an auto-reply.
- Physically put your phone out of reach to avoid temptation.

Step 3: Plan Screen-Free Activities

- Outdoor activities: Walking, jogging, cycling, or hiking.
- Hobbies: Reading, painting, cooking, or writing.
- Quality time: Playing board games, deep conversations, or meditation.

- Mindfulness: Journaling, yoga, or simply enjoying silence.

Step 4: Reflect on Your Experience

- How did you feel without screens?
- Did you feel more peaceful, productive, and present?
- What insights did you gain about your digital habits?

Try this: Go one entire morning without checking social media. Observe how your focus improves.

4. Overcoming Resistance to a Digital Fast

Giving up screens, even for a few hours, can feel uncomfortable at first.

- "What if I miss something important?" → The world won't stop. Let people know in advance.
- "I'll be bored without my phone." → That's a sign of addiction! Find engaging alternatives.
- "I don't have time to unplug." → If you're too busy to take a break, you need one more than ever.

Mindset Shift: Instead of seeing screen-free time as a loss, see it as gaining mental clarity, peace, and real-life experiences.

5. The Long-Term Benefits of Regular Digital Fasting

People who practice Digital Fasting report major life improvements.

More Presence & Awareness – Enjoy life's moments instead of documenting them for social media.
Stronger Relationships – Conversations become deeper and more meaningful.

Increased Productivity – Less distraction means better focus and efficiency.

Greater Control Over Technology – You decide how to use tech instead of being a slave to it.

Final Challenge: Commit to a Digital Fast once a week for a month. Notice how your focus, clarity, and relationships improve.

Learning: Make Digital Fasting a Habit

A Digital Fast isn't about rejecting technology—it's about using it wisely. Just as religious and cultural fasting practices help people regain control over desires, a break from digital overload helps us regain control over our minds.

Key Takeaways:

Unplugging reduces stress, improves focus, and strengthens relationships.

A Digital Fast can last a few hours, a full day, or a weekend.

Plan meaningful offline activities to replace screen time.

Overcome the fear of missing out—real life is happening beyond the screen.

Remember: The best moments in life happen when you are fully present. Take the challenge, unplug, and rediscover the joy of living beyond the screen.

HOW COMPANIES CAN SUPPORT DIGITAL WELLNESS

Workplace Strategies for Reducing Digital Fatigue

> *"Almost everything we do generates data, and every digital interaction affects our well-being. Companies must take responsibility for creating a healthier digital work environment."*
>
> **– Cal Newport**

The Rise of Workplace Digital Fatigue

In today's hyper-connected world, the workplace has become a major source of digital exhaustion. Employees are constantly switching between emails, instant messages, video meetings, and endless notifications. While technology boosts productivity, it also leads to burnout, stress, and mental fatigue.

Did You Know?

- The average employee checks their email over 70 times a day.
- 70% of professionals check work emails after office hours.
- Video call fatigue has increased by 250% since remote work became the norm.

Without proper digital wellness strategies, productivity suffers, mental health declines, and employee engagement drops. Companies that care about their workforce must implement healthy digital habits in the workplace.

1. What is Digital Wellness in the Workplace?

Digital Wellness refers to using technology in a way that enhances productivity without harming mental and physical health. It involves reducing digital overload, setting healthy boundaries, and promoting mindful tech use at work.

Encourages focused, distraction-free work.
Prevents burnout, stress, and eye strain.
Improves work-life balance and job satisfaction.
Enhances overall mental and physical well-being.

Challenge: *How many times do you check your phone or email during work hours?*

2. The Hidden Cost of Digital Overload at Work

- Reduced Productivity – Constant digital interruptions make it harder to focus.
- Increased Stress & Burnout – Overuse of digital tools leads to exhaustion.
- Declining Work-Life Balance – Employees feel pressured to stay connected 24/7.
- Health Issues – Prolonged screen time causes eye strain, headaches, and poor posture.

Example: A study found that employees who receive fewer emails experience lower stress levels and greater job satisfaction.

3. How Companies Can Promote Digital Wellness

A. Implement "No-Notification" Zones & Deep Work Hours

- Set "focus hours" where employees work without digital interruptions.
- Encourage deep work sessions by reducing unnecessary emails and meetings.
- Allow employees to set "Do Not Disturb" modes during critical tasks.

Example: Google implemented "No-Meeting Wednesdays" to allow employees to focus on creative work.

B. Rethink Email & Communication Overload

- Encourage asynchronous communication instead of constant emails.
- Use collaboration tools (Trello, Notion, and Asana) to reduce email clutter.
- Set expectations for response times to prevent after-hours pressure.

Example: Volkswagen stops work-related emails after office hours to protect employees' personal time.

C. Reduce Unnecessary Meetings & Video Calls

- Limit meetings to essential discussions only.
- Set clear agendas and time limits for all meetings.
- Encourage walking meetings or audio calls to reduce screen fatigue.

Example: Shopify reduced meetings by 60% and saw a significant productivity boost.

D. Encourage Screen Breaks & Movement

- Promote the 20-20-20 rule: Every 20 minutes, look 20 feet away for 20 seconds.
- Offer standing desks or encourage short walks between tasks.
- Provide blue light filters for screens to reduce eye strain.

Example: Apple's workplace wellness program includes reminders for employees to move and take breaks.

E. Set Digital Wellness Policies

- Right to Disconnect: Respect employees' off-work hours.
- Tech-Free Meetings: Encourage in-person discussions without screens.
- Flexible Work Hours: Allow employees to choose their most productive hours.

Example: France has a law giving employees the "Right to Disconnect" from work emails after office hours.

4. Creating a Culture of Digital Well-Being

Digital wellness starts with leadership. When companies prioritize digital health, employees feel happier, healthier, and more productive.

Train Managers on Digital Wellness – Teach leaders how to promote healthy tech habits.
Offer Digital Detox Challenges – Encourage employees to take breaks from screens.
Promote Work-Life Balance – Respect employees' time outside work hours.

Final Challenge: *Try a "Tech-Free Friday" where no meetings or emails are allowed after 4 PM.*

Learning: A Healthier Workplace Starts Today

Companies that embrace digital wellness create happier, more engaged employees. By reducing digital fatigue, setting boundaries, and promoting mindful technology use, workplaces can become more productive, balanced, and fulfilling.

Key Takeaways:
Digital wellness reduces stress, improves focus, and boosts productivity.
Companies should implement focus hours, fewer meetings, and email-free times.
Leadership must promote a culture of work-life balance.
Small changes—like screen breaks and mindful communication—lead to a healthier workplace.

Remember: A balanced digital life leads to better work, better health, and better happiness. Starting today!

CHAPTER 27

RECONNECTING WITH NATURE & THE OUTDOORS

The Healing Power of Nature in Breaking Digital Dependency

> *"Look deep into nature, and then you will understand everything better."*
>
> – **Albert Einstein**

The Lost Connection with the Natural World

In today's digital age, people spend more time looking at screens than at the sky. The average person spends over 7 hours a day on digital devices, leading to mental exhaustion, stress, and a disconnect from the real world.

But before the rise of smartphones, humans had a deep connection with nature. Children played outside, families took long walks, and people found peace in the natural world. Now, that connection is fading, replaced by endless scrolling, notifications, and digital distractions.

Did You Know?

- The average child spends less than 30 minutes outdoors daily but over 7 hours on screens.
- Studies show that spending just 20 minutes in nature reduces stress, anxiety, and depression.
- Forest bathing (Shinrin-yoku), a Japanese practice of immersing in nature, lowers cortisol levels and improves mental well-being.

It's time to rediscover nature as a powerful tool for digital detox and mental clarity.

1. Why Nature Heals Digital Exhaustion

Restores Mental Clarity – Nature refreshes the mind, improving focus and creativity.
Reduces Stress & Anxiety – Fresh air and greenery lower stress hormones like cortisol.
Boosts Physical Health – Walking outdoors improves cardiovascular health and posture.
Strengthens Real-Life Connections – Outdoor activities bring families and friends together.

Example: Research shows that just 10 minutes of daily exposure to nature can significantly boost happiness and reduce mental fatigue.

2. Signs You Need a Nature Break

- You feel mentally drained after long screen hours.
- You struggle to concentrate without checking notifications.
- You wake up and check your phone before seeing sunlight.
- You feel disconnected from real-life experiences.
- Your sleep is disturbed due to excessive screen exposure.

If you relate to these, nature can be your best remedy.

3. Practical Ways to Reconnect with Nature

A. Take Daily Digital-Free Walks

- Go for a morning or evening walk without your phone.
- Observe trees, birds, and the sounds of nature to stay present.
- Walk barefoot on grass (earthing) to absorb natural energy.

Challenge: Try a 30-minute walk without your phone and notice how you feel.

B. Weekend Nature Escapes

- Plan hiking, camping, or beach trips with friends or family.
- Visit national parks, forests, or lakes to immerse in nature.
- Try gardening or spending time in a backyard or park.

Example: Many companies now encourage "Work from the Woods" retreats to boost employee creativity.

C. Outdoor Exercise & Meditation

- Practice yoga or meditation in a natural setting.

- Do your morning stretches on a balcony or garden.
- Try cycling, running, or swimming instead of gym workouts.

Example: Studies show that outdoor workouts are more effective in reducing stress and improving energy levels than indoor workouts.

D. Limit Screen Use in Natural Spaces

- Set a rule: No screens during outdoor activities.
- Keep your phone on silent or airplane mode when in nature.
- Use nature as a replacement for digital entertainment.

Challenge: Spend one hour in nature without touching your phone.

E. Try a Digital Detox Nature Retreat

- Join a nature retreat or silent meditation camp to disconnect.
- Visit places with no network or Wi-Fi to force digital detox.
- Go on a camping trip where you cook, explore, and connect with nature.

Example: The "Digital Detox Camp" movement is growing, where people spend days in nature without screens.

4. Making Nature a Part of Daily Life

Start your day by watching the sunrise instead of checking your phone.
Replace social media scrolling with watching birds, clouds, or the sky.
Take work breaks by stepping outside instead of checking notifications.
Spend evenings stargazing, walking, or sitting in nature.
Keep house plants or a mini garden to stay connected with greenery.

Learning: Nature as the Ultimate Reset

Nature is the original therapist, stress reliever, and digital detox solution. The more time you spend outdoors, the less control technology will have over your mind.

Key Takeaways:
Spending time in nature reduces digital addiction and improves mental health.
Simple activities like walking, hiking, and outdoor meditation can break digital dependency.
A daily dose of nature restores focus, creativity, and emotional well-being.

Challenge: Take a 24-hour digital fast and spend it entirely outdoors. See how refreshed you feel!

BUILDING A LONG-TERM DIGITAL DETOX PLAN

Sustainable Strategies for a Tech-Healthy Future

> *"The best way to predict your future is to create it."*
>
> **– Peter Drucker**

Why a Long-Term Digital Detox Plan Matters

Most people attempt short-term digital detoxes—a weekend off social media, a day without a phone—but soon return to old habits. Without a structured, sustainable plan, digital addiction creeps back in.

A long-term digital detox is about more than just taking a break. It's about building habits that allow you to use technology without being controlled by it. Instead of quitting screens completely, the goal is to create a balanced relationship with digital devices.

Did You Know?

- 80% of people who try a digital detox return to excessive screen time within a month.
- The average person spends 44 years of their life looking at screens.
- People who actively manage their screen time report higher happiness, focus, and productivity.

It's time to take control and design a long-term strategy for a healthier digital life.

1. The Pillars of a Sustainable Digital Detox Plan

A long-term digital detox isn't about quitting technology—it's about using it wisely. Here's how:
Awareness – Recognizing unhealthy screen habits.
Boundaries – Setting clear limits on digital use.
Replacement – Finding fulfilling real-world activities.
Consistency – Turning small changes into lifelong habits.

Challenge: *What's one digital habit you want to change forever?*

2. Step-by-Step Guide to a Long-Term Digital Detox

Step 1: Self-Assessment – Where Do You Stand?

- Track your daily screen time (use apps like Digital Wellbeing, Moment, or Rescue Time).
- Identify your biggest digital distractions (social media, emails, streaming, etc.).
- Ask yourself: *Do I control my device, or does it control me?*

Exercise: Write down your top 3 screen-related habits you want to change.

Step 2: Set Clear Digital Boundaries

- Create screen-free zones (e.g., no phones at dinner or in the bedroom).
- Set time limits on social media (use built-in app timers).
- Establish "No-Notification" periods during deep work or family time.

Example: People who stop using their phone one hour before bed improve their sleep quality by 68%.

Step 3: Replace Screen Time with Real-Life Activities

- Swap social media scrolling for reading, exercise, or outdoor walks.
- Replace online entertainment with hobbies like painting, music, or sports.
- Spend more time with friends and family in person, not just online.

Challenge: Try replacing 30 minutes of screen time with a hobby daily for a week.

Step 4: Implement Regular Digital Fasts

- Daily: Set a 1-hour no-screen rule every evening.
- Weekly: Have a tech-free day (Digital Sunday).
- Monthly: Take a weekend retreat without screens.
- Yearly: Go on a one-week digital detox vacation.

Example: Billionaires like Bill Gates take "Think Weeks" where they disconnect from tech and focus on deep thinking.

Step 5: Build a Tech-Healthy Environment

- Remove unnecessary apps that waste time.
- Disable auto-play features on streaming platforms.
- Use grayscale mode on your phone to make screens less addictive.
- Keep your phone away from your bed to avoid late-night scrolling.

Example: People who delete one addictive app (like Instagram or TikTok) for a month report lower stress and increased productivity.

Step 6: Involve Family & Friends

- Make digital detox a group challenge with friends.
- Plan screen-free social activities (game nights, outdoor trips).
- Educate children on healthy screen habits from an early age.

Example: Families who adopt a "No Phones at Dinner" rule have stronger relationships and better communication.

3. Overcoming Challenges & Staying Consistent

Common Struggles & How to Fix Them:

Fear of Missing Out (FOMO) → Remind yourself that real life is happening outside the screen.
Boredom without Screens → Fill your time with hobbies, reading, and real-world experiences.

Work Demands Too Much Digital Time → Use focus modes, batch emails, and deep work techniques.
Relapse into Old Habits → Have an accountability partner or track your progress.

Tip: Write a Digital Detox Contract for yourself, listing your rules, goals, and consequences for breaking them.

4. The Long-Term Benefits of a Digital Detox Plan

If you commit to a sustainable digital detox, you will:

Regain focus and eliminate mindless scrolling.
Improve mental health by reducing stress and anxiety.
Sleep better without blue light disturbing your rest.
Strengthen relationships by being present with people.
Boost productivity by eliminating distractions.

Challenge: Start your 30-Day Digital Detox Plan today! Write down 3 habits to change and take action.

Learning: A Tech-Healthy Future Starts Now

Technology is a powerful tool, but only if we use it with intention. A long-term digital detox isn't about quitting technology—it's about mastering it.

Key Takeaways:

A successful digital detox plan is about balance, not restriction.
Small changes—like screen-free dinners and digital fasting—lead to big results.
The more you control your digital habits, the more control you have over your life.

Are you ready to reclaim your time, focus, and mental clarity? Start today!

CHAPTER 29

A LIFE OF PRESENCE & PURPOSE

The Ultimate Reward of a Digital Detox Lifestyle

> *"Wherever you are, be all there."*
>
> **– Jim Elliot**

The True Cost of Digital Overload

We live in an age where we are more connected than ever, but often feel disconnected from ourselves, our loved ones, and the world around us. The constant stream of notifications, endless scrolling, and digital distractions rob us of our ability to be present in the moment.

Many people wake up and check their phones before they even step out of bed. Meals are eaten while staring at screens, conversations are interrupted by notifications, and precious life moments slip away unnoticed.

But what happens when you break free from digital addiction? What does life look like when you are truly present?

The answer is a life of awareness, fulfillment, and deep human connections—a life with purpose.

Did You Know?

- The average person spends over 10 years of their life on social media.
- Constant screen exposure lowers emotional intelligence and real-world social skills.
- People who practice mindful digital use report greater happiness and stronger relationships.

1. What Does It Mean to Live a Life of Presence?

Presence is the ability to be fully engaged in the current moment—without distractions. It means:

Deep conversations instead of half-listening while scrolling

Mindful eating instead of watching TV while having meals

Enjoying nature instead of capturing every moment for social media

Being with loved ones instead of checking notifications

A digital detox helps you reclaim this presence, bringing clarity, joy, and real human connections.

Challenge: *Try spending an entire day fully present—no distractions, no multitasking. Experience how it feels.*

2. The Power of Purpose: Why It Matters

Living with purpose means aligning your time and energy with what truly matters. Instead of wasting hours on mindless scrolling, you invest in:

Personal Growth – Reading, learning new skills, or deep thinking
Relationships – Spending quality time with family and friends
Health & Well-Being – Exercising, meditating, or enjoying nature
Passions & Creativity – Writing, painting, playing music, or volunteering
Career & Productivity – Focusing on meaningful work without digital distractions

Example: Studies show that people who limit social media use to 30 minutes per day experience greater happiness, reduced stress, and increased life satisfaction.

3. How to Maintain a Life of Presence & Purpose

A successful digital detox isn't just about cutting screen time—it's about building a lifestyle where technology serves you, not controls you.

A. Define Your Priorities

- What matters most in your life? Family? Health? Learning? Creativity?
- Write down your top 3 life priorities and commit to giving them more time.

Exercise: *Compare how much time you spend on screens vs. your true priorities.*

B. Set Digital Boundaries for a Purposeful Life

- No phones during meals – Focus on the food and conversation.
- Dedicated work blocks – No social media during deep work hours.
- Morning mindfulness – Start the day without a screen.
- Tech-free evenings – Spend time reading, journaling, or reflecting.

Example: People who follow a "No Screens 1 Hour After Waking & Before Sleeping" rule report better mental clarity and deeper sleep.

C. Cultivate Mindful Tech Use

- Use tech with intention, not as an escape.
- Unfollow unnecessary accounts that don't add value to your life.
- Turn off non-essential notifications to reduce distractions.
- Schedule digital detox breaks (daily, weekly, and yearly).

Challenge: *Try a "No-Scroll Weekend" and use that time for meaningful real-world activities.*

D. Find Meaningful Alternatives to Digital Distractions

- Replace screen time with face-to-face connections.
- Engage in hobbies and creative activities that bring joy.
- Spend more time in nature for mental clarity and relaxation.

Example: Many people who reduce digital distractions find themselves reading more books, picking up old hobbies, and reconnecting with forgotten passions.

4. The Ultimate Rewards of a Digital Detox Lifestyle

If you embrace a life of presence and purpose, you will:

Feel more in control of your time and attention.
Experience deeper and more meaningful relationships.
Have more energy and mental clarity for creative thinking.
Enjoy a sense of fulfillment instead of digital burnout.
Live with intention, focusing on what truly brings joy and growth.

Final Challenge: *What's one habit you can change today to live a more present and purposeful life? Start now!*

Learning: Reclaiming Your Life from Digital Distractions

A digital detox isn't about eliminating technology—it's about reclaiming your time, focus, and purpose. When you learn to control your digital habits, you gain the freedom to fully experience life.

Key Takeaways:

Presence = Living fully engaged in each moment.
Purpose = Spending time on what truly matters.
Technology should serve you, not steal your life.

Remember: Every moment spent mindlessly scrolling is a moment lost. Choose to be present. Choose to live with purpose.

THE FUTURE OF TECHNOLOGY & HUMAN WELL-BEING

How to Create a Balanced Digital Future Without Addiction

> *"Technology is a useful servant but a dangerous master."*
>
> **– Christian Lous Lange**

1. The Crossroads of Technology & Humanity

We are standing at a crucial turning point. Technology has given us unimaginable advancements—instant communication, limitless knowledge, and AI-powered tools that make life easier. Yet, it has also led to mental exhaustion, digital addiction, and a loss of real-world connection.

The question is no longer "Can we live without technology?" but rather "How can we use technology without losing ourselves?"

If we continue mindlessly consuming digital content, we risk becoming a generation of distracted, anxious, and disconnected individuals. But if we make conscious choices, we can create a balanced future where technology serves human well-being rather than destroys it.

Did You Know?

- The average person spends 7+ hours a day on screens, leading to reduced focus and creativity.
- Studies show that excessive social media use is linked to depression and anxiety.
- Countries like Denmark and Finland are already implementing "Digital Well-Being Policies" to protect citizens from digital burnout.

So, how do we build a future where technology enhances our lives without enslaving us?

2. Rethinking Our Relationship with Technology

We must shift from being passive consumers of technology to intentional users. Instead of allowing screens to dictate our lives, we need to set clear boundaries and use technology in ways that:

Enhance productivity and knowledge
Support mental and physical health
Strengthen human relationships
Promote creativity and deep thinking

Challenge: *Think about one area in your life where technology is controlling you. How can you take back control?*

3. Key Principles for a Balanced Digital Future

To ensure that future generations use technology responsibly, we must focus on the following:

A. Ethical & Human-Centered Technology

- Tech companies should design products that prioritize well-being rather than addiction.
- Regulations should limit manipulative algorithms that exploit human psychology.
- AI should be used ethically to enhance, not replace, human decision-making.

Example: Companies like Apple and Google are integrating digital well-being features (screen time tracking, app limits, etc.) into their devices.

B. Digital Literacy & Awareness

- Schools and workplaces should teach digital wellness as part of education.
- People need to understand how social media and apps manipulate behavior to make informed choices.
- Parents should educate children about responsible screen use from an early age.

Example: Finland has introduced media literacy programs to help students critically analyze digital content.

C. Mindful & Minimalist Tech Use

- Use technology only when necessary, instead of as a default activity.
- Designate screen-free zones at home and work.
- Adopt "digital minimalism"—keeping only the apps and tools that add value.

Example: People who practice "email batching" (checking emails only twice a day) reduce stress and improve productivity.

D. Rebuilding Real-Life Connections

- Prioritize face-to-face conversations over virtual interactions.
- Encourage communities to spend time together without screens.
- Create social norms where "no-phone zones" become the standard.

Example: Many restaurants now offer discounts to customers who keep their phones away during meals.

E. Implementing Regular Digital Detox Practices

- Adopt "Digital Fasting" days to unplug from screens.
- Encourage workplaces to implement tech-free hours.
- Spend more time in nature, hobbies, and real-world experiences.

Example: Japan has introduced "Forest Bathing" (Shinrin-Yoku) programs to help people reconnect with nature and reduce digital fatigue.

4. The Future We Can Create Together

The future of technology and human well-being is in our hands. If we make intentional choices today, we can create a world where:

Technology empowers people rather than enslaves them.

Children grow up with healthy screen habits and real-world experiences.
Digital spaces promote truth, creativity, and mental well-being.
People live with presence, purpose, and deep human connections.

Final Thought: Technology should be a tool that enhances human potential—not a force that diminishes it.

Are you ready to shape a future where technology serves YOU, not the other way around?

CONCLUSION: A WAKE-UP CALL TO RECLAIM OUR MINDS AND SHAPE A BETTER TOMORROW

As we reach the final pages of this book, I invite you to pause—not just to reflect, but to awaken.

This is not just another self-help guide. It is a mirror held up to our times, revealing a hard truth: we are losing ourselves to devices designed not to empower us, but to consume us. What began as tools to connect the world has quietly morphed into powerful systems engineered to manipulate attention, shape behavior, and monetize every second of our lives.

And perhaps the most alarming part? **Most people don't even realize it.**

We are surrounded by a silent epidemic—**an addiction so normalized, it goes unnoticed**. Children are being raised on screens, not stories. Teenagers are trading dreams for dopamine hits. Adults—working professionals, parents, educators—are drifting away from purpose, unable to focus, constantly distracted, and emotionally exhausted. It's everywhere. And it's getting worse.

But we are not just fighting bad habits. We are standing against **an empire of tech giants** whose profits are directly tied to how distracted, addicted, and emotionally reactive we are. Their algorithms don't serve your wellbeing—they serve their bottom line. They are not incentivized to help you focus. They profit when you scroll, click, consume, and repeat.

That's the uncomfortable truth. And yet, here you are—still reading, still searching, still willing to take back control. And that gives me hope.

Because in a world where the majority has chosen convenience over consciousness, **you must dare to stand out**. You must become the exception.

This book is my humble contribution to that resistance. A small, determined step toward reclaiming what matters most—our time, our minds, our relationships, and our peace. Through *Swipesober*, I am not asking you to abandon technology. I am asking you to master it, before it masters you. To use it with wisdom, not as an escape. To protect your attention like you protect your health—because attention **is** your mental health.

And as a responsible citizen of your family, your workplace, your nation—you must ask yourself:

Where is your attention going? Who is shaping your thoughts? And are you living by your own will—or being led by algorithms?

Because the consequences of mass distraction are far more dangerous than we imagine.

A distracted engineer may design weak foundations.
A distracted surgeon may make a fatal error.
A distracted teacher may fail to ignite young minds.
A distracted leader may misguide an entire nation.

A distracted society is a vulnerable society.

That's why this mission matters. A healthy mind doesn't just lead to a healthy life—it leads to a better world. *Focused individuals build focused families. Focused families create resilient communities. And resilient communities shape a powerful nation.*

This is my first book. It may not be perfect. But my intention is. My heart is in these pages. My mission is clear—to awaken minds, restore balance, and inspire change.

And I am not walking away after this.

To every reader who resonates with this message, I extend my hand. Let's stay connected. Let's grow together. Let's build a movement of awareness, discipline, and digital integrity. One family at a time. One mind at a time.

The future belongs to those who are present.And presence begins when we silence the noise.
Thank you for joining me on this journey.
Let's rise together. Let's live mindfully.
Let's become **Swipesober**—not just for ourselves, but for generations to come.

— *With gratitude and purpose,*

Milap Oza